PUFFIN BOOKS

PUZZLER'S A TO Z

How many states are there in the USA?
In what film does an alien want to phone home?
What sort of creature was Pegasus?

These are just some of the many questions posed by the quizzes in this wonderfully original and varied book. In addition there are puzzles of every kind to suit a range of abilities and interests.

Whether you work your way through this alphabet of puzzles and quizzes or just dip into them at random, you're sure to find hours of stimulating entertainment.

Colin Gumbrell lives in Horsham, Sussex, and was a bookseller before becoming a full-time writer. He is a former British Scrabble champion.

PUFFIN BOOKS

Illustrated by Mike Gordon

Colin Gumbrell

Puzzler's **A** to **Z**

PUFFIN BOOKS

Published by the Penguin Group
27 Wrights Lane, London W8 5TZ, England
Viking Penguin Inc., 40 West 23rd Street, New York, New York 10010, USA
Penguin Books Australia Ltd, Ringwood, Victoria, Australia
Penguin Books Canada Ltd, 2801 John Street, Markham, Ontario, Canada L3R 1B
Penguin Books (NZ) Ltd, 182–190 Wairau Road, Auckland 10, New Zealand

Penguin Books Ltd, Registered Offices: Harmondsworth, Middlesex, England

First published 1989
10 9 8 7 6 5 4 3 2 1

Text copyright © Colin Gumbrell, 1989
Illustrations copyright © Mike Gordon, 1989
All rights reserved

Filmset in 11pt Linotron Palatino by
Rowland Phototypesetting Ltd, Bury St Edmunds, Suffolk
Made and printed in Great Britain by
Cox and Wyman Ltd, Reading, Berks.

Puzzles

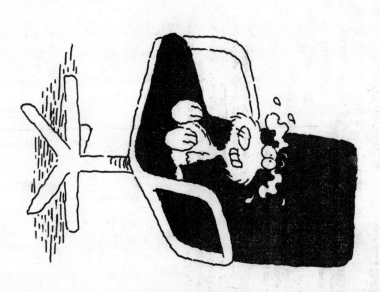

...WHAT WORD GOES BEFORE SHOD, CAST AND CUT?

ALPHABETICAL WORD-QUEST

Welcome to your first assignment! All you have to do is find twenty-six words, each of which is four letters long, in the word-quest below. It's an alphabetical quest because every word begins with a different letter of the alphabet (and, for good measure, every word ends with a different letter of the alphabet as well). The words run in all directions – forwards, backwards, downwards, upwards, and even diagonally – but always in a straight line.

And if you can find all the words from A to Z, award yourself an A+ for An Amazing Achievement at the outset of this Alphabetical Adventure!

ANAGRAM ANSWERS

An anagram is a rearrangement of the letters of one word so that they spell another word. WHO, for example, is an anagram of HOW. What could be simpler? (The answer to that question must be PRELIMS – short for preliminaries – which is, of course, an anagram of SIMPLER.)

Now that the prelims are over, it's over to you. Each of the following ten questions has a one-word answer, an anagram of the word or words given in capital letters in the question. Even if you've never done this sort of thing before, your RAWNESS shouldn't stop you from working out some of the ANSWERS!

1. What THING is often moonlit? Night

2. From what kind of tree does a FIR CONE come? conifer

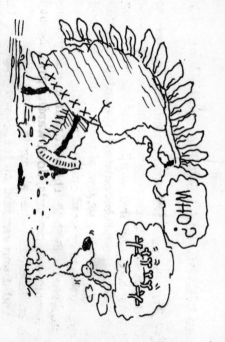

7

3. When did Jules VERNE go to the moon?
   Never

4. Which boat should you not take out on the OCEAN?
   Canoe

5. What should you pay to someone who wields a SCEPTRE?

6. What was God's REACTION to the problem of having nothing to do? CREATION

7. Which town DOMINATES part of Kent?

8. What was the crime of the SENATOR who conspired against Julius Caesar?

8

9. For what do you need to know the PRECISE ingredients?

10. Who may be found in THE CLASSROOM?

AS I WAS GOING . . .

As I was going to St Ives,
I met a man with seven wives;
And every wife had seven sons;
But they were not the only ones,
For every son had seven sisters!
Bewildered by so many misters
And by so many misses too,
I quickly cried: 'Bonjour! Adieu!'
And hurried to another street,
Away from all their trampling feet.
Now, here's the point that puzzles me yet:
Just how many people had I met?

ASTRONOMY QUIZ

1. Which is the largest planet in the solar system?

   Jupiter

2. What travels at 186,000 miles per second?

   Light

3. Which Polish astronomer created a stir with his revolutionary theory that the Earth moves round the Sun?

   Nicholas Copernicus

4. If the southern lights are Aurora Australis, what are the northern lights?

5. When does a solar eclipse take place?

6. To which constellation, named after a mythical hunter, does the red star Betelgeuse belong?

   Orion

7. Which long-tailed heavenly body comes within sight of the Earth once every seventy-six years, and was last seen in 1986?

8. What is a light-year?

9. What is the common name for a region of space, created by a collapsed star, from which not even light can escape?

10. Which is the nearest star to the Earth?

BATTLES

Can you match these ten famous battles with the years in which they took place?

1.	Agincourt	a.	1066
2.	Blenheim	b.	1314
3.	Naseby	c.	1415
4.	Battle of Britain	d.	1485
5.	Hastings	e.	1645
6.	Waterloo	f.	1685
7.	Bosworth Field	g.	1704
8.	Sedgemoor	h.	1805
9.	Bannockburn	i.	1815
10.	Trafalgar	j.	1940

BIRD QUEST

A flock of feathered friends are flying, running and waddling through this word-quest. In all, there are thirty-eight to be spotted; and all you need to succeed is an eagle eye!

```
Y B B O H G U O H C A L G F
T R E K C E P D O O W L N L
E H L I N E T T O R U I E
M A G P I E L L C T E G W R
U W B O F R N I U G N E P T
D K S L F O L A R R O R A S
N I T R A M A U L O R U L E
I J A Y H C R Q E B E T I K
F N R A C S K I W H L S R
F A L C O N O B T N S U N O
U W I D G E O N I E E V I T
P S N E V A R W O R R A P S
L E G D I R T R A P D N E T
```

BLACK OR WHITE?

Here are ten sentences; a word or part of a word has been left out from each sentence. Your job is to fill in the missing word, which in every case is either BLACK or WHITE.

1. The President of the USA lives in the _white_ House.
2. Anyone who's making a profit is said to be in the _____.
3. _____ jack is the name of a card game.
4. Something that's useless may be called a _____ elephant.
5. The Dominicans are also known as _____ Friars.
6. The Carmelites are also known as _____ Friars.
7. The Penny _Black_ was the first adhesive postage stamp.
8. Termites are sometimes called _____ ants.
9. The _Black_ widow is a venomous American spider.
10. _The Sword in the Stone_ was written by T. H. _____.

13

BOOK QUIZ

1. Who wrote two books about a boy called Charlie Bucket?

   Roald Dahl

2. Who had a friend called Colonel Dedshott, a housekeeper called Mrs Flittersnoop and five pairs of glasses?

3. In *The House at Pooh Corner* by A. A. Milne, for whom was the house at Pooh Corner built?

   Eeyore

4. Which detective solved the mystery of a gigantic hound in Devonshire?

   Sherlock Holmes

5. In which book was a magic ring found by Bilbo Baggins?

   The Hobbit

6. Who escaped from prison by disguising himself as a washerwoman?

   Toad

7. Which English city was visited by a unicorn in *Elidor* by Alan Garner?

   Manchester

8. Who was the brother of Flopsy, Mopsy and Cottontail?

9. In *The Lion, the Witch and the Wardrobe* by C. S. Lewis, what were the names of the four Pevensie children who found their way into Narnia?

10. Which of the boys in the workhouse asked for more?

CAPITAL ANAGRAMS

I think Oliver Twist was misunderstood. When he asked for more, he didn't really want a second helping of gruel. What he was trying to say was that he wanted to leave the workhouse and travel far away, to a beautiful foreign city. But, being Oliver, he got his letters in a twist, and asked for that city's anagram instead. Can you put him on the right road, then keep travelling and unravelling the other eleven anagrams of capital cities all over the world?

1. MORE
2. SOLO
3. GOALS
4. UNITS
5. PAIRS
6. ROBINIA
7. MAIL
8. LOUSE
9. HASTEN
10. ANIMAL
11. BAULK
12. CASCARA

COL'S COLLECTION

Every word in this collection begins with the letters COL.

1. COL the young horse: COL_
2. COL the old king: COL_
3. COL the coal-miner: COL_ I _ _ _
4. COL the New World's discoverer: COL_ _ _ _ _
5. COL the settler: COL_ _ _ _ _
6. COL the army officer: COL_ _ _ _
7. COL the gigantic statue: COL_ _ _ _ _
8. COL the total breakdown: COL_ _ _ _ _
9. COL the workmate: COL_ _ _ _ _
10. COL the perforated strainer: COL_ _ _ _ _
11. COL the crash: COL_ _ _ _ _ _
12. COL the pillar: COL_ _ _
13. COL the American state: COL_ _ _ _ _
14. COL the monkey: COL_ _ _ _
15. COL the tummy upset: COL_ _ _ _ _ _ _ _ _

HE SEEMS TO BE UNDER SOME KIND OF STRAIN!

VET

17

COUNTY QUEST

If you can count twenty English counties, you'll have achieved a perfect score!

```
W R I E R I H S E H C E
L A N C A S H I R E R R
Y E R R U S P L I I T I
L L A W N R O C H D E H
T H S S I X E S S U S S
E C O R D C N E P R R K
R M I P O L A S A A M O
O B T C W A N E H M O Y
D R N N O V E D R I S H
E I E K L O F R O N R M
L A K E D N A X E S S E
```

CROSS-NUMBER PUZZLE

Down

A. Year of the Great Fire of London B. Degrees in a circle C. The _____ dollar question E. *The _____ Dalmatians*, by Dodie Smith G. Weeks in a year J. Year of the battle of Blenheim L. Emergency number N. Top score with three darts O. Year of the Spanish Armada P. A gross Q. Five cubed S. In Roman numerals, CC U. The PM's house number

Across

B. Days in a leap year   D. Age when you may be given the key of the door   F. Year of the Gunpowder Plot   H. Seven squared   I. _____ *Leagues Under the Sea*, by Jules Verne   J. A cricket team   K. Methuselah's age   M. Bond number   N. Year when George V became king   P. Year when World War I ended   R. In *The Hitchhiker's Guide to the Galaxy*, the Ultimate Answer   T. One score   V. Year of the battle of Bosworth Field   W. The speed of light in miles per second

19

DAYS QUIZ

1. When is St Valentine's Day?

2. From midnight to midnight, how many minutes are there in one day?

3. What is the title of John Wyndham's story about an invasion of the Earth by huge stinging plants?

4. Which day of the week is named after an ancient Italian god of agriculture?

5. It is the last day before a fast, and known in French as Mardi Gras. What is it called in English?

IT'S STOPPED!

6. According to superstition, what will happen if it rains on St Swithin's Day?

ILL rain for forty days

7. If today is Monday, on which day was the day before yesterday the day after tomorrow?

THursday

8. Which day is an international distress signal?

Mayday

9. What is the connection between 1 March, 17 March, 23 April and 30 November?

10. How many months of the year have twenty-eight days?

DEFINITION ALPHABET

On the left are twenty-six words, from A to Z; on the right are twenty-six definitions, also from A to Z. Can you match the words with their proper definitions?

A.	ARCHIPELAGO	a.	Ancient ship with five sets of oars
B.	BANDICOOT	b.	Beads used as money
C.	CENTAUR	c.	Cigar-shaped airship
D.	DAVENPORT	d.	Dark-coloured layer of cloud
E.	EUPHORIA	e.	Early form of bicycle
F.	FUMAROLE	f.	Fear of foreigners
G.	GLADIOLUS	g.	Group of islands
H.	HECTARE	h.	Hole in a volcano
I.	IONOSPHERE	i.	Indian rat
J.	JODHPURS	j.	Joyous feeling
K.	KELPIE	k.	King of ancient Egypt
L.	LEVERET	l.	Leopard-like cat
M.	MATZO	m.	Mythical monster
N.	NIMBO-STRATUS	n.	North American wood-pecker
O.	OCELOT	o.	Ornamental writing-desk
P.	PHARAOH	p.	Plant with sword-shaped leaves
Q.	QUINQUE-REME	q.	Quadrilateral figure
R.	ROENTGENO-GRAPHY	r.	Riding-breeches

S.	SAPSUCKER	s.	Small guitar with four strings
T.	TRAPEZIUM	t.	Ten thousand square metres
U.	UKULELE	u.	Unleavened bread
V.	VELOCIPEDE	v.	Veil worn by Muslim women
W.	WAMPUM	w.	Water-sprite in the form of a horse
X.	XENOPHOBIA	x.	X-ray photography
Y.	YASHMAK	y.	Young hare
Z.	ZEPPELIN	z.	Zone of the upper atmosphere

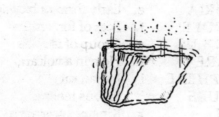

DOUBLETS

A doublet is a pair of words of the same length, the first of which has to be changed into the second, in a given number of steps, by altering one letter at a time. A genuine word must be made at every step.

Example: Change CAT into DOG in three steps.

Answer:
CAT	or	CAT
1. COT		1. COT
2. DOT		2. COG
3. DOG		3. DOG

Now try these:

1. Change BOY into MAN in three steps.

2. Change FOUL into FAIR in three steps.

3. Change RISE into FALL in four steps.

4. Change HAIR into BALD in four steps.

5. Change DRY into WET in five steps.

6. Change LOSS into GAIN in five steps.

7. Change PIGS into PORK in five steps.

8. Change HEADS into TAILS in five steps.

9. Change WORK into PLAY in seven steps.

10. Change GIRL into LADY in seven steps.

EASY CROSSWORD

You shouldn't need too much expertise to fill in the answers with a great deal of Es!

Across
1. Always
2. A slippery fish
3. A fencer's sword

Down
1. Cost

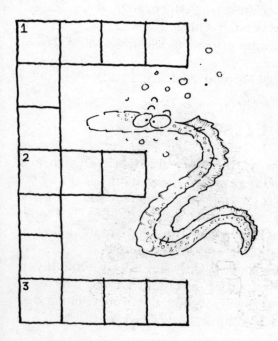

ELIZABETH, EMILY OR ESTHER?

Can you find the proper names for the people described below?

1. Miss Rantzen, a television presenter. _____
2. Miss Brontë, the sister of Charlotte and Anne. _____
3. Mrs Fry, a prison reformer. _____
4. Miss Taylor, a film star. _____
5. An Old Testament heroine. _____
6. Mrs Barrett Browning, an English poet. _____
7. Miss Dickinson, an American poet. _____
8. The owner of Bagpuss. _____
9. Miss Summerson, in Dickens's *Bleak House*. _____
10. Mrs Gaskell, a novelist. _____

ENGLISH TEST

There are many thousands of words in English, and nobody could possibly know them all. But how many words, of three or more letters, can you make out of the seven-letter word ENGLISH? Proper nouns (like Neil, Nigel and Nile) are not allowed; neither are plurals and abbreviations.

Any score above twenty-five is very good. If you can beat my total of thirty-four words, which are listed in the answers section, then your command of ENGLISH is nothing short of excellent!

EXPEDITIONS QUIZ

1. Who was the leader of the first expedition to reach the South Pole, on 14 December 1911?

2. Who was the leader of the second expedition to reach the South Pole, on 18 January 1912?

3. Sir Francis Drake sailed round the world in a ship called the *Pelican*. What was the ship later renamed?

4. On 21 July 1969, who took 'one small step for a man, one giant leap for mankind'?

5. Which Greek hero led an expedition to recover the Golden Fleece?

6. According to Edward Lear, who 'went to sea in a sieve'?

7. Which HMS went all the way to Ujiji just to find a doctor?

8. Vasco da Gama was the first navigator to round

the Cape of Good Hope and sail to India. What was his nationality?

9. Why did Edmund Hillary and Norgay Tensing feel on top of the world on 29 May 1953?

10. Who discovered the North Pole while out with his friends on an Expotition?

EYE-RHYMES

Eye-rhymes are words that look as if they rhyme with each other, but actually don't (like TO and GO, for example). Here are twelve pairs of them, but by rearranging them you can make twelve pairs of real rhymes.

Where? Here!

1. COLLEGE, ALLEGE
2. CONCISE, EXPERTISE
3. DISGRACE, PALACE
4. FAHRENHEIT, DECEIT
5. MALICE, TWICE
6. PEAR, HEAR
7. QUAYS, WAYS
8. REPEAT, GREAT
9. REPHRASE, CASE
10. WEDGE, KNOWLEDGE
11. WEIGHT, HEIGHT
12. WEIR, HEIR

FILM QUIZ

1. In which film did Danny Kaye sing 'Inchworm', 'Thumbelina' and 'Wonderful Copenhagen'?

2. In *The Wizard of Oz*, which character wanted a heart?

3. 'Here's another nice mess you've gotten me into!' Who was always saying that, and to whom was he always saying it?

4. Which film was about an alien who wanted to phone home?

5. The Muppets' first film was called *The Muppet Movie*. What was the title of their second film?

6. Which actor told Sam to 'play it' in *Casablanca*?

7. What was the name of the Wookie in *Star Wars*?

8. Which film was about an elephant who could fly?

9. Which level-headed character was first portrayed on film by Boris Karloff?

10. In Walt Disney's *Snow White and the Seven Dwarfs*, what were the names of the seven dwarfs?

FIRST DIVISION

By drawing three lines, can you divide this figure into three triangles and two squares?

FISH QUEST

Sea fish, freshwater fish, flatfish and shellfish: forty-two delicious fish wish to be fished out of this – and that's official!

```
S S A B D A C S H A R K
I T N D A C E T A K S S
L A U B L E R E K C A M
E R T R C S O L E O L E
E P G I G N I L M D E L
K S A L N E Q U A D S T
I L R L I N O M L A S U
P T U O R T E N C H U B
E B T U R B O T A S M I
R A M A E R B A R B E L
C D R A H C L I P A R A
H C A O R B L E N N Y H
```

34

FOUR BY FOUR

This crossword may not be as easy as it seems. You'd be wise, perhaps, to make a rough copy before you seize the chance to fill the answers in.

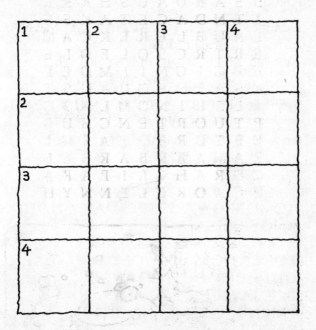

Across
1. Oceans
2. Is in debt
3. Vegetables from a pod
4. Knowledgeable

Down
1. Imitate
2. Newsworthy material
3. Ape
4. Reproduce

GATECRASHERS

Here are eight sets of words. Four items in each set belong together because of some common factor, but the fifth is a gatecrasher and has no right to be there. Can you identify the gatecrashers and throw them out?

Example A: GALA, BAZAAR, ALMANAC, FÊTE, PANDA.

Answer: FÊTE. E is its only vowel, whereas A is the only vowel in the others.

Example B: FIRE, TOAD, MILK, FROG, SNOW.

Answer: TOAD. The others can all take the suffix MAN.

1. TOMORROW, YESTERDAY, NATION, KNOCK, HEALTH.
2. SYZYGY, LYNX, LINKS, RHYTHMS, FLY.
3. EDUCATION, SEQUOIA, BOUNDARIES, OUTSIDER, OUTDISTANCE.
4. BEE, JAY, CUE, EYE, BUY.
5. FRIEND, WAR, PARTNER, ALLY, BATTLE.
6. THROUGH, CLUE, TROUGH, QUEUE, COUP.
7. TOOL, HAMMER, SAW, REWARD, POT.
8. RANGE, SCOPE, VISION, PATH, GRAPH.

GEOGRAPHY QUIZ

1. Which is the highest mountain in the United Kingdom?

2. Which island off the coast of Australia was formerly called Van Diemen's Land?

3. Which state in the USA is the furthest west?

4. Which country has the largest population in the world?

5. Cape Horn is the southernmost extremity of which continent?

6. Which is the longest river in the United Kingdom?

7. Which country completely surrounds the republic of San Marino?

8. By what collective name are Superior, Huron, Michigan, Erie and Ontario commonly known?

9. Which country has a Worm's Head in the south and a Great Orme's Head in the north?

10. Which sea's surface is more than a thousand feet below sea level?

GREAT CROSSWORD

Across

3. _____ the Great, Empress of Russia
5. Great ___: a gorilla, perhaps
6. Great ___: a dog
8. The Great ___: a constellation
9. _____ the Great, Macedonian general
12. The five Great _____ of North America
13. Great ___: a bell in Oxford
14. The Great _____, one of Henry VIII's ships

Down

1. Great ___! Sir Walter?
2. ___ the Great, King of Judaea
4. 'Great _____', by Charles Dickens
7. The Great _____, Brunel's largest steamship
8. Great _____: an island
10. The Great ___, better known as the Mediterranean
11. The Great ___, 1914–18

I'm going as one of the great heads of Europe!

39

HIS AND HERS

Every word contains the letters HIS or HER, as indicated after the clues.

1. HIS past: HIS<u>TORY</u>
2. HER brave man: HERO
3. HIS emblem of Scotland: _THIS___
4. HER fruit: _HER___
5. HIS card game: _HIS_
6. HER female ancestor: _ _ _ _ _ _ _ _HER
7. HIS sideburns: _HIS_ _ _ _
8. HER educator: _ _ _ _HER
9. HIS *Treasure Island* ship: HIS_ _ _ _ _ _
10. HER Indian tribesman: _HER_ _ _ _
11. HIS supporter of royalty: _ _ _ _ _ _HIS_
12. HER light boxer: _ _ _ _HER_ _ _ _ _
13. HIS sculptor's tool: _HIS_ _
14. HER detective: _HER_ _ _ _ _ _ _ _ _
15. HIS greenfly: _ _HIS
16. HER temperature taker: _HER_ _ _ _ _ _ _ _

40

HOMONYM HUNT

Homonyms are words that sound the same but have different meanings. (They may or may not have the same spelling.) In the following sentences, the homonyms have been replaced by their meanings and are given in capital letters. Can you restore the homonyms to their rightful places?

Example: We went to LOOK AT the OCEAN.
Answers: SEE, SEA.

1. Kate CONSUMED a plate of MORE THAN SEVEN dates. _____, _____
2. The sea is the LOCATION in which to find A YELLOW-SPOTTED FLATFISH. _____, _____
3. His enemies TREMBLE at the name of the ARAB CHIEF. _____, _____
4. Talking AUDIBLY is not PERMITTED. _____, _____
5. Have you eaten a FRUIT? No, I've eaten a COUPLE! _____, _____
6. The ANTELOPE truly WAS AWARE that the moon was FRESH. _____, _____, _____
7. The priest gives COMMENDATION and SUPPLICATES. _____, _____
8. No BLOOD-SUCKING INSECT can RUN

41

AWAY FROM the circus. _____, _____

9. The dog under the LAUREL tree beside the INLET OF THE SEA loves to BARK at the CHESTNUT-COLOURED HORSE. _____, _____, _____, _____

10. The PERFUME he DISPATCHED was worth a HUNDREDTH OF A DOLLAR. _____, _____, _____

11. Wherever I WANDER, there's no place like ITALY'S CAPITAL. _____, _____

12. Don't SPLIT ASUNDER, but UNITE! _____, _____

HOW MANY?

1. How many metres are there in a kilometre? _____

2. How many States are there in the USA? _____

3. How many petals does a buttercup have? _____

4. How many decades are there in a century? _____

5. How many black squares are there on a chess-board? _____

6. How many people did Jesus feed with seven loaves and a few small fishes? _____

7. How many faces has a dodecahedron? _____

8. How many pennies are there in a hundred pounds? _____

9. How many musicians are needed to play a nonet? _____
10. How many steps are there in the title of a book by John Buchan? _____
11. How many players are there in a volleyball team? _____
12. How many humps has a Bactrian camel – one hump or two? _____

IN OPPOSITION

If you were asked to give the opposite of the word CORRECT, your answer would undoubtedly be INCORRECT. Can you, however, give the correct opposites of these adjectives?

1. POSSIBLE
2. LEGIBLE
3. RESPONSIBLE
4. VISIBLE
5. MEASURABLE
6. FLAMMABLE

43

I.S.

I.S. is short, initially speaking, I suppose, for In Short. What are the following abbreviations short for?

1. A.W.O.L.
2. B.B.C.
3. C.I.A.
4. D.S.O.
5. E.E.C.
6. F.T.
7. G.M.T.
8. H.R.H.
9. I.T.N.
10. J.P.
11. K.O.
12. L.V.
13. M.O.T.
14. N.S.P.C.C.
15. O.E.D.
16. P.T.O.
17. Q.P.R.
18. R.N.L.I.
19. S.R.N.
20. T.A.
21. U.F.O.
22. V.T.R.
23. W.R.V.S.
24. Y.H.A.

ISLANDS

Can you identify these islands (not all drawn to the same scale)?

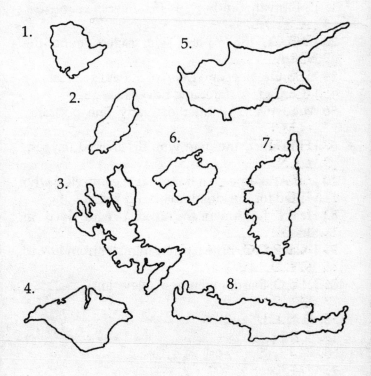

1.

2.

3.

4.

5.

6.

7.

8.

JAMES, JOHN OR JOSEPH?

Which are the Josephs, which are the Johns, and whose name's James?

1. J. Bunyan, author of *The Pilgrim's Progress*. _____

2. J. Cook, the captain who sailed round the world. _____

3. J. Donne, poet and Dean of St Paul's. _____

4. J. Conrad, seafarer and novelist. _____

5. Augustus J., painter of many fine portraits. _____

6. J. Priestley, the man who discovered oxygen. _____

7. J. of Arimathea, an honourable counsellor who waited for the kingdom of God. _____

8. Henry J., American novelist who lived in Sussex. _____

9. J. Callaghan, British prime minister from 1976 to 1979. _____

10. J. Logie Baird, inventor of television. _____

JEWEL QUEST

Eighteen precious and semi-precious stones are buried in the grid. Unearth them all, an' jewel be rich!

```
D J S O J A S P E R C
Y R A M E T H Y S T H
N I P D N O M A I D R
O H P G E L A P O R Y
D T H A Z Y Z Z U S S
E N I R A M A U Q A O
C I R N S P B E R Y L
L C E E O N Y X U L I
A A N T U B B Y T O T
H Y C A R B U N C L E
C H A D L A R E M E N
```

JUST JOKING

A quiz to be taken with a pinch of salt.

1. Why is there so little honey in Birmingham?

2. Which Scandinavian city is in the middle of Czechoslovakia?

3. What kind of pet can you tread on without hurting it?

4. On which side of the human body is the liver?

5. What is the worst time of day to pay a visit to a dentist?

6. Which cheese is made backwards?

7. What has wings and flies, but doesn't?

8. Why do only 325 days belong to the year?

9. What was Sherlock Holmes's favourite tree?

10. How many ears did Davy Crockett have?

KEY WORDS

Every answer contains the letters KEY.

1. A bird and also a country: _ _ _KEY
2. A ball game played with sticks: _ _ _KEY
3. Animal ridden by Don Quixote's squire: _ _ _KEY
4. A footman: _ _ _KEY
5. Another footman: _ _ _ _KEY
6. Rider in a horse-race: _ _ _KEY
7. Irish spirit that's often drunk: _ _ _ _KEY
8. Something found at the apex of an arch: KEY_ _ _ _ _
9. Mouse who looks nothing like a mouse: _ _ _KEY
10. A record player: _ _ _ _ _ _ _KEY
11. A mammal and also a hammer: _ _ _KEY
12. The blueback salmon: _ _ _KEY_
13. A Hole near Wells in Somerset: _ _ _KEY
14. What's played by a truant: _ _ _KEY
15. A town in Buckinghamshire: _ _ _ _ _ _ KEY_ _ _

KINGS QUIZ

1. Which King of England lost his head on 30 January 1649?

2. Who was the father of King Solomon?

3. Which King, who ruled Denmark and Norway as well as England, proved that he was not all-powerful by failing to turn the tide?

4. In a pack of cards, which of the four Kings has half as many eyes as the others?

5. Which King of England, known as Rufus because of his red hair, was killed by a stray arrow in the New Forest?

6. Which King was a tennis player who won six singles titles at Wimbledon?

7. Which name belonged to eighteen Kings of France?

8. Which King of England was twice divorced and thrice a widower?

9. Which King's last words, according to Shakespeare, were 'A horse! a horse! My kingdom for a horse!'?

10. Which King was shot down by aeroplanes from the top of a New York skyscraper?

Kong

KNIGHTS OF THE ROUND TABLE

Eight of King Arthur's knights are seated round the Round Table, bewitched by a wicked spell cast upon them by a horrible hag. In a daze, the knights' names have been turned into anagrams, the beginnings and endings of which are indicated by the lines marking out the radius of the table. Can you conjure up eight good spells, to restore the right names to the knights and thus rid them of their hag-ridden bewilderment?

LEGS ELEVEN

Every word in this puzzle includes the letters LEG.

1. An unhistorical story: LEG_ _ _
2. A body of Roman soldiers: LEG_ _ _
3. Place of learning: _ _ _LEG_
4. A daily newspaper: _ _LEG_ _ _ _
5. Easy to read: LEG_ _ _ _
6. Loyalty: _ _LEG_ _ _ _ _
7. In football, the opposite of promotion: _ _LEG_ _ _ _ _
8. A bean, for example: LEG_ _ _
9. Unlawful: _ _LEG_ _ _
10. Graceful: _LEG_ _ _
11. Sleight of hand: LEG_ _ _ _ _ _ _ _

LETTER-SPELLS

If BD stands for BEADY, what do the following groups of letters stand for?

1. CD   _____
2. IC   _____
3. NV   _____
4. SA   _____
5. AT   _____
6. XS   _____
7. XLNC   _____
8. OBCT   _____
9. KN   _____
10. FEG   _____

A... U C D GOL'FISH?

LIMERICKS' LAST LINES

Here are some limericks which have lost their last lines. Supply your own – then turn to the back to see how close yours are to mine.

1. There was an old man from Darjeeling,
   Who developed a spidery feeling:
   When friends came to call,
   He would crawl up the wall,

   _____.

2. A hopeful young Frenchman, intent
   On swimming his way into Kent,
   Just couldn't get over
   The white cliffs of Dover –

   _____.

3. A bearded old German, called Marx,
   Ate capital picnics in parks:
   He would bark like a pup,
   Then bite everything up –

   _____.

4. A space-craft from some remote planet
   Came down with a thump upon Thanet;
   The alien crewmen
   All croaked, 'How d'you do, men!' –

   _____?

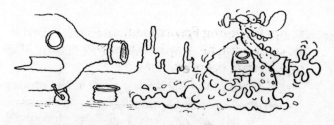

5. In the green-tinted twilight of Italy,
   Leonardo da Vinci cried bitterly:
   'Your smile is too faint –
   And I've run out of paint!'

   _____.

LITERATURE TEST

How many words, of three or more letters, can you make from the ten-letter word LITERATURE? As in the case of ENGLISH, proper nouns and abbreviations are not allowed.

If you can find over a hundred, you're doing very well (and showing admirable patience, too!). I've listed 130 words in the answers section; but dedicated detective-work in dictionaries would no doubt reveal quite a few more. In any case, you're sure to find many more words in LITERATURE than you did in ENGLISH – take my word for it!

LUCKY DIP

You may not know the answers but you can always trust to luck in this quiz and take a shot in the dark!

1. Is the number of people known to have died in the Great Fire of London (a) about 2,000; (b) 472; (c) over 5,000; or (d) 6?
2. Are the islands of Langerhans (a) on the moon; (b) off the coast of Denmark; (c) in the human body; or (d) in *Gulliver's Travels* by Jonathan Swift?
3. Was the zip-fastener invented by (a) Benjamin Franklin; (b) Whitcomb L. Judson; (c) Alexander Graham Bell; or (d) Franco Zipparelli?
4. Is St Crispin the patron saint of (a) farmers; (b)

shoemakers; (c) carpenters; or (d) fishermen?

5. Is K the symbol for the chemical element (a) potassium; (b) krypton; (c) kurchatovium; or (d) sodium?

6. Are angels on horseback (a) star clusters in the Crab Nebula; (b) characters in the Book of Revelation; (c) oysters and bacon on toast; or (d) the Royal Canadian Mounted Police?

7. The first film in the Pink Panther series was called *The Pink Panther*. Was the second one called (a) *The Return of the Pink Panther*; (b) *The Revenge of the Pink Panther*; (c) *The Pink Panther Strikes Again*; or (d) *A Shot in the Dark*?

8. Does the name Cloudesley Shovel belong to (a) a village in Devon; (b) an English admiral of the seventeenth century; (c) an animal in one of the tales of Beatrix Potter; or (d) a prototype mechanical plough?

9. Is the sequoia (a) the Californian redwood tree; (b) a rare South American bird with beautiful green plumage; (c) a hot wind that blows over the Sahara Desert; or (d) a dance similar to the polka?

10. Was Boris Karloff's real name (a) Archibald Leach; (b) Harry Webb; (c) William Pratt; or (d) Boris Karloff?

MAGIC SQUARES

1. Enter the numbers 2, 3, 5, 6, 8 and 9 in such a way that every line of three (including the two diagonals) adds up to fifteen.

2. Enter the numbers 1, 3, 4, 5, 6, 8, 12, 13 and 14 in such a way that every line of four (including the two diagonals) adds up to thirty-four.

MIXED FRUIT AND VEGETABLES

Can you restore these edible anagrams to their natural condition?

1. LUMP
2. REPLAYS
3. WEEDS
4. CHEAP
5. KEEL
6. MILE
7. NOMADS
8. AMONG
9. CHARIOT
10. ARGENTINE

MONEY MATTERS

Can you match the units of currency with the countries in which they are current?

1. Zloty	a. Australia
2. Peseta	b. Czechoslovakia
3. Shekel	c. Greece
4. Dollar	d. India
5. Rouble	e. Israel
6. Koruna	f. Italy
7. Rupee	g. Japan
8. Drachma	h. Poland

9. Yen   i. Russia
10. Lira   j. Spain

11. Without looking, can you say in which direction Queen Elizabeth II faces on British coins?

12. If a suit and tie together cost £115, and the suit costs exactly £100 more than the tie, what is the price of each?

13. If a cucumber and a half cost 45p, how many cucumbers can you buy for a pound and a half?

14. A bag contains two pounds' worth of 5p, 10p and 50p coins. The number of 5p coins multiplied by the number of 50p coins equals the total number of coins in the bag. How many coins of each kind are there?

15. On which current British coin is there a portrait of Britannia?

MYTHS AND LEGENDS QUIZ

1. What was the name of King Arthur's sword?

   _____

2. Which monster, with the body of a man and the head of a bull, was kept in a labyrinth built by Daedalus for King Minos of Crete?

   _____

3. What was the Roman name for the Greek goddess Aphrodite? _____

4. Which knight of the Round Table was the father of Sir Galahad? _____

5. What was the city of the Norse gods called?

   _____

6. Which mythical Arabian bird burned itself to death once every five hundred years, and was then reborn out of its own ashes?

   _____

7. Which war dragged on for ten years, and ended when a wooden horse was dragged inside a city's walls? _____

8. In Celtic mythology, which island in the Irish Sea was the home of the god Manannan?

   _____

9. What kind of animal was Pegasus?

   _____

10. Who was the son of a woman called Igraine and a man called Uther Pendragon?

    _____

NATIONAL ANAGRAMS

The capitalized words in each sentence are nations in consternation. Can you show enough determination to rearrange them into their proper combinations?

1. This might be the best nation in which to set a Biblical television SERIAL.

2. If the population of this nation stood in a line, the resulting CHAIN would be much longer than the Great Wall.

3. King Arthur's mother IGRAINE never visited this nation.

4. Most of the people of this nation are members of the LAITY.

5. High up in the Andes, the air of this nation is PURE.

6. This is a nation INLACED by the sea.

7. The inhabitants of this nation may well be IN A GLOOM.

8. A dazzling RAY IS what Paul saw on the road to this nation's capital.

9. This is a nation where people rarely dance the RUMBA.

10. Is this a nation for COLD TANS?

11. Very few DARK MEN are natives of this nation.

12. The easiest way to cross the mountains of this nation is in a PLANE.

13. Do the rulers of this nation wear REGALIA?

14. Financial WIZARDS LENT lots of money to this nation's banks.

15. RAIN is rare in this nation.

NATURE TRAIL

Here is an extract from Gerry's diary, recounting the events which followed an unsuccessful fishing trip with his friend Marcel. The extract contains the names of fifty-one trees, flowers and creatures which Gerry appears to have noticed that day. None of them, however, are named directly. Some are wholly concealed within one word, while others begin in one word and end in another, ignoring all punctuation.

How many of the items on Gerry's nature trail can you track down? The first two are done for you.

April <u>the ninth</u>
It <u>was</u> pretty late, a light breeze blew, and over-head a shimmering haze lay across the sky. Two walking fishermen, Marcel and I, nets in our hands, wandered towards our camp. 'I only caught a blue-bellied pair,' I sighed. 'Not so bad. Gerry,' Marcel muttered. 'I landed a

rusty arrow, a feather, one enormous egg, and a beer can too.' The arrow, anyway, is a crisp arrow,' I said. His face darkened. 'I'm allowed to grouch, aren't I?' he growled. 'Ye wouldn't if,' I began – but swallowed my words in horror. For at that moment, in the south, rushing storm-clouds arose and with urgency pressed towards us. 'Marcel, amble not!' I cried. 'I'm not terribly keen on a night in gale-force winds!' As if in chariots of fire, the two of us ran swiftly, he at heroic speed. 'We'll soon be out of this drab, bitter weather!' he yelled. Eerily, snow dropped from the sky; and Marcel, arching his back, got soaked. At last, to be sure, a gleam of light guided us to a tavern. There we sat down, ravenously hungry, to a delicious meal. 'Marcel,' I said jollily, 'that was a wholly memorable day!'

NUMBERS QUIZ

1. Which telephone number should you dial to call the operator?

2. Of which number is a sufferer from triskaidecaphobia morbidly afraid?

3. If you divide the number of men under the command of the grand old Duke of York by the number of people fed by Jesus with five loaves and two fishes, what number is the result?

4. How can you write 1009 in such a way that it looks like a jumble?

5. What are the first five prime numbers?

6. Which fractional number, when read upside-down on an electronic calculator, appears to be a greeting (if you ignore the decimal point)?

7. In four years' time I shall be twice as old as I was eleven years ago. How old am I now?

8. Using each of the digits from 1 to 9 once, can you write down three three-digit numbers, making the second number exactly double the first, and the third number exactly three times the first?

9. In bingo, which number is top of the house?

10. If the question is 20 8 5 17 21 5 19 20 9 15 14, what is the answer?

ODD ONE OUT

Which is the odd one out in each of these groups – and why?

1. Haddock, hake, shark, whale, whiting.
2. Stitch, slip, point, cover, gully.
3. Ostrich, emu, penguin, cassowary, puffin.
4. Inspector, Constable, Sargent, Whistler, Turner.
5. Macaroni, cannelloni, tarantella, lasagne, spaghetti.
6. Minim, maxim, semi-breve, crotchet, quaver.
7. Genesis, Judges, Matthew, Daniel, Proverbs.
8. Washington, Pennsylvania, Cleveland, Hoover, Lincoln.
9. Flintlock, cannon, fetlock, muzzle, pastern.
10. Mercury, Mars, Neptune, Jupiter, Venus.

OF MICE AND MEN

MICE and MEN are, of course, the plurals of MOUSE and MAN. But do you know the plurals of these words?

1. GOOSE   _____
2. MOOSE   _____
3. MONGOOSE   _____
4. WOODLOUSE   _____
5. TALISMAN   _____
6. PHENOMENON   _____
7. DEER   _____
8. LENS   _____
9. SPECIES   _____
10. PLATYPUS   _____

OFF WITH ITS HEAD!

Every answer consists of two words. Behead the first word by removing its initial letter, and the second word is instantly discovered.

Example: Behead a backbone to make a tree.
Answer: SPINE, PINE.

1. Behead an insect to make a snake. _____, _____

2. Behead a dog to make a bird of prey.
_____, _____

3. Behead an odd number to make it not odd.
_____, _____

4. Behead a wind instrument to make one with strings. _____, _____

5. Behead pigs to make a drink. _____,
_____

6. Behead Odysseus to make a foul smell.
_____, _____

7. Behead a fiend to discover what he is.
_____, _____

8. Behead nothing to make more than nothing.
_____, _____

9. Behead Long John Silver to make him furious.
_____, _____

10. Behead the occupier of the White House to make the occupier of any house. _____,
_____

11. Behead a marine creature to make a pound.
_____, _____

12. Behead a man to make beer. _____,
_____

13. Behead Jack's friend to make her unwell.
_____, _____

14. Behead the Iron Duke to make the Duke of Jazz.
_____, _____

15. Behead the chief Norse god and make a fearful noise. _____, _____

ORCHESTRAL QUEST

Can you conduct a successful quest for twenty-five musical instruments, most of which (though not all) might be found in an orchestra?

```
A R M U I N O H P U E L
B A S S O O N A I P E A
E T S P A M U R D I M B
N I A O B O E P P P P M
O U B O U B E S T S E Y
H G E L T E N I R A L C
P Y L O N E I C U L G O
O C B C K T L H M T N R
X E U C R U O O P E A N
A L O I V L I R E R I E
S L D P A F V D T Y R T
G O R E N O B M O R T S
```

OUT OF ORDER

Can you organize the following groups into the right order – either chronologically or in descending order of rank, as appropriate?

1. *TUDOR
   MONARCHS*
   Edward VI   Henry VIII
   Elizabeth I   Mary I
   Henry VII

2. *ROMAN EMPERORS*
   Tiberius
   Nero
   Claudius
   Caligula
   Augustus

3. *WARS*
   The American War of
     Independence
   The Boer War
   The Crimean War
   The English Civil
     War
   The First World War
   The Hundred Years'
     War
   The Wars of the Roses

4. *ARMY RANKS*

Brigadier	Lieutenant-Colonel
Captain	Major
Colonel	Major-General
Lieutenant	

5. *NAVAL RANKS*
   Admiral
   Admiral of the Fleet
   Captain
   Commander
   Commodore
   Rear-Admiral
   Vice-Admiral

6. *RAF RANKS*
   Air Commodore
   Air Vice-Marshal
   Flight Lieutenant
   Flying Officer
   Group Captain
   Squadron Leader
   Wing Commander

71

PARTNERS APART

Can you bring the proper partners together again?

1. ROMEO and JUDY

2. GILBERT and ALBERT

3. BATMAN and GARFUNKEL

4. LAUREL and CLYDE

5. PUNCH and ISOLDE

6. VICTORIA and ROBIN

7. TOM and JULIET

8. TRISTAN and HARDY

9. SIMON and SULLIVAN

10. BONNIE and JERRY

PERPLEXED PEOPLE

Here are some anagrams of famous people's names, together with a clue or two to help you work out who is who.

1. THE GRATE FLARED – and that's why his cakes went up in flames! (6,3,5)

2. CHILDREN'S CAKES – which Mr Bumble never gave to the boys in the workhouse. (7,7)

3. I BAT ON HAM – but it's easier on a cricket pitch. (3,6)

4. NO, I CRAVE QUIET – in other words, I'm not amused. (5,8)

5. TINY BLONDE – who created Big Ears! (4,6)

6. I'LL MAKE A WISE PHRASE – like 'All's Well That Ends Well'. (7,11)

7. OPEN? NO, APART ON ELBA – where he was sent in the year before the opening of his last campaign. (8,9)

8. CARRY ON HOUND TALE – which is exactly what he did. (6,5,5)

9. DANISH SIR'S AN ENCHANTER – that's all you need to know. (4,9,8)

10. YANKY DANE – in other words, an American actor who played the Danish sir. (5,4)

PLACE NAMES

The answers to the clues are the names of places in the British Isles. First, find the names – then see if you can place them correctly in the crossword.

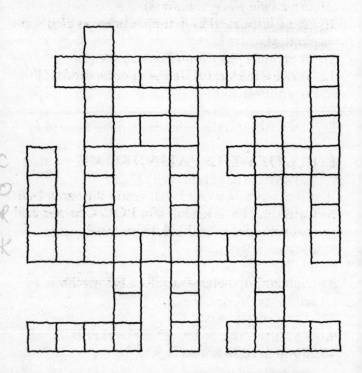

1. A place east of London that's sounding like a dog (7)
2. A woolly place in Wales (8)
3. An Irish place that stops a bottle (4)

4. A wooden place in Kent (4)
5. A soft county in Northern Ireland (4)
6. A Lancashire place that's a bomber (9)
7. An Irish place that rhymes (8)
8. A filthy-sounding Hebridean island (4)
9. An edible place in Kent (8)
10. A Hebridean island that sounds as if it's on high (4)
11. A Scottish place found in a candle (4)
12. A place in Hampshire that may be fired (10)

POP GOES THE PALINDROME

A palindrome is a word that reads the same both forwards and backwards – like POP. Can you find the palindromes to fit these definitions?

1. Something that goes under a baby's chin.

2. Pertaining to a city.

3. Something that's done.

4. Turned into a god.

5. A female sheep.

6. The hole of a needle.

7. A joke – or something to stop you telling it!

8. An Eskimo's canoe.

9. Even.

10. A musical note.

11. The moment when the morning ends.

12. Someone who lives in a convent.

13. A seed found in a fruit.

14. The high deck at the stern of a ship.

15. More blushing.

16. A giver of the kiss of life, perhaps.

17. Part of a helicopter.

18. Icelandic hero-tales.

19. Places over which bishops have authority.

20. Add up the score (it may be a little one!).

PREPOSTEROUS PROVERBS

The second half of each proverb has attached itself to the wrong first half, with ridiculous results. Please restore proverbial propriety!

1. Too many cooks flock together

2. A rolling stone saves nine

3. Birds of a feather spoil the broth

4. A bird in the hand laughs longest

5. Many hands shouldn't throw stones

6. A stitch in time has a silver lining

7. A friend in need is worth two in the bush

8. Every cloud gathers no moss

9. People who live in glass houses make light work

10. He who laughs last is a friend indeed

QUEENS QUIZ

1. Which Queen of England was the daughter of Henry VIII and Anne Boleyn?

2. Which Queen led a revolt against the Romans

and is commemorated by a statue, which stands near the Houses of Parliament in Westminster and shows her standing in a chariot drawn by reinless horses?

3. In Snakespeare's *A Midsummer Night's Dream*, is the queen of the fairies (a) Titania; (b) Cynthia; (c) Gloriana; or (d) Queen Mab?

4. Which Queen was loved by Julius Caesar and Mark Antony?

5. Who 'went stamping about, and shouting, "Off with his head!" or "Off with her head!" about once in a minute' – and in which book?

6. Which Queen was born at 17 Bruton Street in London on 21 April 1926?

7. Where is the queen always more powerful than the king?

8. Which Queen, having unwisely suggested that the common people could eat cake, was eventually guillotined in Paris in 1793?

9. Which Queen's name has been given to an African lake, an Australian state and an English railway station?

10. Which Scottish football league club plays its home matches in Dumfries?

QUESTIONS OF LOGIC

The answers to most of these questions are easy, obvious and logical – as soon as you know what they are!

1. A big Eskimo and a little Eskimo went fishing together. The little Eskimo was the big Eskimo's son; yet the big Eskimo was not the little Eskimo's father. How do you explain that?

2. A squirrel gathered six ears of corn and hurried off to add them to his secret hoard inside a hollow tree. On the way he dropped two of the ears and ate a third. How many ears did he still have when he finally reached the tree?

3. A train leaves London for Edinburgh at ten o'clock in the morning. Half an hour later, another train leaves Edinburgh for London. If both trains are travelling at the same speed, which of them will be nearer to London when they meet?

4. Two fathers and two sons went to the cinema. None of them were allowed in for less than the full admission price, yet they only paid the price of admission for three. Why did they get away with it?

5. A farmer was standing in a field, together with half a dozen horses, a dozen dogs and six dozen sheep. How many feet were there in the field?

6. I have two coins which together add up to the value of sixty pence, yet one of them is not a fifty-pence piece. What are the two coins?

7. Two men were on trial for murder. The jury found one of them guilty and the other not guilty. By law, the judge ought to have sent the guilty man to prison; yet he was compelled, by law, to set both the innocent and the guilty man free. How could that be?

8. If an aeroplane were to crash right on the border between East Germany and West Germany, in which country, according to international law, would the survivors be buried?

QUOTATION QUOTA

Who said the following, and in which stories?

1. 'Oh my ears and whiskers, how late it's getting!'

2. 'Man-Pack and Wolf-Pack have cast me out. Now I will hunt alone in the Jungle.'

3. 'You don't know about me, without you have read a book by the name of *The Adventures of Tom Sawyer*, but that ain't no matter.'

4. 'Believe me, my young friend, there is *nothing* – absolutely nothing – half so much worth doing as simply messing about in boats.'

5. 'Alas, poor Yorick. I knew him, Horatio.'

6. 'Do you believe in fairies? If you believe, clap your hands!'

7. 'How would you like to live in Looking-glass House, Kitty?'

8. 'Many's the long night I've dreamed of cheese – toasted, mostly.'

9. 'But, soft! what light through yonder window breaks? It is the east, and Juliet is the sun.'

10. 'All for one, one for all.'

RATS LIVE ON . . .

Just as a palindromic word reads the same forwards and backwards, so a palindromic sentence reads the same forwards and backwards (regardless of punctuation). The first-ever palindromic sentence is thought to have been spoken by the very first man, when he introduced himself to Eve (herself a palindrome) by saying: 'Madam, I'm Adam.'

Here are some more sentences, meant to be palindromic, which have been cut off at or around the half-way point. Can you complete them?

  1. Rats live on _____
  2. Don't _____
  3. Dennis, I _____
  4. Pupils _____
  5. Name not _____
  6. Delia's never _____
  7. Air an _____
  8. Spit slid off a _____
  9. Pat a red nut _____
 10. Sums are not set as _____

RHYME TIME

Each line of the rhyme is a separate clue. There are ten words to find – and it's all up to you.

1. It rhymes with time and ends with b;
2. It rhymes with Sioux and means to see;
3. With life she rhymes, a female spouse;
4. A bird, a grumble – rhymes with house;
5. It rhymes with lost, it's cold as ice;
6. It's heaven, and it rhymes with nice;
7. Rhyming with lead, it means to go;
8. Rhyming with lead, it slides on snow;
9. This rhymes with sirs, but isn't his;
10. This rhyme for worse is all there is.

85

RIVER QUEST

Test your knowledge of the world's waterways in this quest. Thirty-two rivers are flowing through the grid – fifteen of them belonging to the British Isles, the others to the rest of the world.

```
N O V A N R E V E S I
O N O Z A M A E U P O
N I L E D M X S P E Y
N I G E R E N I H R Y
A M A N O R S O R C A
H T N I J S E M A H T
S I G E I E E D T R R
E G E S T Y N E E H E
E R S A W H U D S O N
T I B E R I O L T N T
M S N O D A N U B E Y
```

SECOND DIVISION

By drawing nine straight lines, can you divide this figure into eight equal parts?

SEMI-SPELLS

The following words are only half-spelt. Can you fill
in the holes to make the words whole?

1. In a frenzy: _M_K
2. An Oriental market-place: _ _ _AAR
3. A flower: DAH_ _ _
4. One who never forgets: _LEPH_ _ _
5. A hot, spouting spring: GEY_ _ _
6. Nonsense (as spoken by turkeys?):
    _ _ _ _ _ _DEGOOK
7. A large lizard: IGU_ _ _
8. Riding breeches: _DHPU_ _
9. A piece of cloth that may be handy:
    KE_ _ _ _EF
10. A cat with tufted ears: L_ _X
11. An aromatic seed used as a spice: _ _ _MEG
12. Something made with eggs: _MELE_ _ _
13. David was a famous one: PSA_ _ _ _T
14. A quaking bog: _ _ _GMIR_
15. Every song should have one: _H_ _HM
16. Hard wheat-grains used in puddings:
    SEMO_ _ _ _
17. You're doing well if you go from this to this:
    _ _ _ _NGTH
18. Useful when it's wet: UM_ _ _ _LA
19. A good place for a powwow: _ _ _WAM
20. A heavenly belt: ZOD_ _ _

SILLY SIMILES

Can you sort these scrambled similes into a semblance of sense?

1. As cool as Punch _____ a cucumber
2. As bald as the hills _____ coot
3. As mad as the day is long _____ a ladder
4. As pleased as a picture _____ Punch
5. As old as gold _____ the hills
6. As happy as a hatter _____
7. As dead as a cucumber _____ dodo
8. As good as a coot _____
9. As honest as a dodo _____ sand-boy
10. As pretty as a sand-boy _____ picture

SOME SUMS

1. $E + E + E = WE$.
   What are the digits represented by W and E?

2. Write down four nines in a sum that adds up to exactly a hundred.

3. $A + B + C = D$.
   $A \times B \times C = D$.
   What are the digits represented by A, B, C, and D?

4. Write down six ones in a sum that adds up to twelve.

5.   AAA
     BBB
     CCC
    ─────
    BAAC

In this addition sum what are the digits represented by A, B and C?

6. Write down eight eights in a sum that adds up to exactly a thousand.

7.   AEB
      DF
     CGA
      BE
    ─────
    FDCB

In this addition sum, what are the digits represented by A, B, C, D, E, F, and G?

8. 987654. 876543. 765432. 654321. 543210.
   Which sign should you insert into each of the above five sets of numbers to create five sums all leading to the same answer?

SPORTS QUIZ

1. In which sport does play begin with a bully-off?

   Hockey

2. Which county cricket team plays its home matches at Kennington Oval?

   Surrey

3. If you were using woods and irons, which sport would you be playing?

   golf

4. In snooker, what is the total value of the six coloured balls – yellow, green, brown, blue, pink and black?

   27

5. In which sport do national teams compete for the Davis Cup?

   Lawn Tennis

6. At which racecourse is the Grand National run?

   Aintree

7. When football's first World Cup competition was held in 1930, were the winners (a) Argentina; (b) Brazil; (c) Italy; or (d) Uruguay?

   Urguay

8. In which sport are hoops and a mallet needed?

   Croquet

9. Which annual race takes place between Putney and Mortlake?

10. In which sport does play end when the referee calls no-side?

    Rugby football

TAILS THEY LOSE

Every answer consists of two words. Find the first word, cut off its tail, and you'll find the second word left behind.

> Example: Cut the tail off a backbone to make a whirl.
> Answer: SPINE, SPIN.

1. Cut the tail off a hog to make a constrictor.
   _____, __ ____

2. Cut the tail off a muffler to make a wound's mark. _____, _____

3. Cut the tail off an amphibian to make it fresh.
   _____, _____

4. Cut the tail off a host to make a black bird.
   _____, _____

5. Cut the tail off a fool to make a friend. _____,
   _____

6. Cut the tail off a long-billed bird to make a cut.
   _____, _____

7. Cut the tail off a wading bird to make someone like Superman. _____, _____

8. Cut the tail off a fish to make a vehicle. _____,
   _____

9. Cut the tail off Pluto to make a smoothing tool.
   _____, _____

10. Cut the tail off a country to make its money.
    _____, __ ____

11. Cut the tail off a tailpiece to make a fish. _____,
_____

12. Cut the tail off a burrowing animal to make an emblem. _____, _____

13. Cut the tail off a duck to make a meal. _____,
_____

14. Cut the tail off a tailed heavenly body to make it draw near. _____, _____

15. Cut the tail off a coney to make a Jewish teacher.
_____, _____

TEN CAPITALS

Name the capital cities of the following nine countries – then rearrange the nine capitals' capitals to arrive at the tenth capital.

1. CANADA: _____
2. CHILE: _____
3. DENMARK: _____
4. FINLAND: _____
5. JAPAN: _____
6. NORWAY: _____
7. PORTUGAL: _____
8. URUGUAY: _____
9. ZAIRE: _____
10. _____

THIRD DIVISION

The least number of pieces into which a circle can be divided by six straight lines is seven (as illustrated in figure 1). If each of the lines crosses all the others, then the least number of pieces has to be twelve (as, for example, in figure 2). But what is the *greatest* number of pieces into which a circle can be divided by six straight lines?

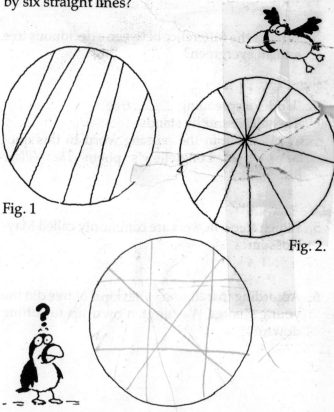

Fig. 1

Fig. 2.

TREE QUIZ

1. What was the name of the tree from which Adam and Eve took the forbidden fruit?

2. After being defeated at the battle of Worcester in 1651, in what kind of tree did Charles II hide?

3. What is the difference between a deciduous tree and an evergreen?

4. 'Under a spreading _____ tree
   The village smithy stands'.
   Can you fill in the missing word in this quotation from Longfellow's poem *The Village Blacksmith*?

5. Which tree's flowers are commonly called May-blossom?

6. According to tradition, what kind of tree did the young George Washington own up to cutting down?

7. On which of these trees would you expect to see catkins in the spring – (a) hazel; (b) ash; (c) willow; (d) oak?

8. What is the main distinguishing feature of trees grown by the Japanese art of bonsai?

9. 'Of all the trees that are in the wood', which one, in the words of the carol, 'bears the crown'?

10. What can you tell about a tree from the concentric rings inside its trunk?

TRUE OR FALSE?

1. Lawn tennis was originally called sphairistike. _____

2. Alfred Nobel, founder of the Nobel Prizes, was also the man who invented dynamite. _____

3. Centipedes have exactly a hundred legs. _____

4. The month of July is named after Julius Caesar. _____

5. Bombay duck is a kind of fish. _____

6. George Eliot, the novelist, was the father of T. S. Eliot, the poet. _____

7. Both Charlie Chaplin and Stan Laurel were born in England. _____

8. The planet Earth is a perfect sphere. _____

9. The ball-point pen was invented by a Hungarian called Biro. _____

10. John Wayne's real name was Marion Morrison. _____

11. Land's End is the most southerly point of Great Britain. _____

12. The koala bear is not a true bear. _____

13. Gustav Holst was a Swedish composer whose best-known work is *The Planets*. _____

14. William Shakespeare had a son called Hamnet. _____

15. The line followed by Hadrian's Wall marks the present-day border between England and Scotland. _____

UNCLUED CROSSWORD

Although there are thousands of possible solutions to this little crossword, I have two particular words in mind for it. All you have to do is look, and think – and see if you can think along the same lines as I do!

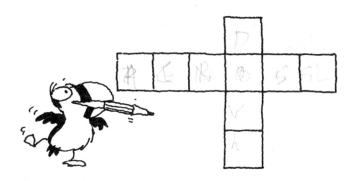

UNITED NATIONS

The answer to each clue is the name of a nation. The last letter of each nation is also the first letter of the next, so that all sixteen nations are united in a chain which, beginning in the top left-hand corner of the diagram, leads inwards in a clockwise spiral to finish in the centre.

It's up to you to unite the nations, to avoid a breakdown in communications!

1. A nation that sounds as if it needs a meal.
2. A nation with a coastline on the Adriatic Sea.
3. A nation which borders on Greece and the one above.
4. The nation of Haydn, Mozart and Schubert.
5. A nation noted for a kind of hound.
6. A nation where plenty of fjords are found.
7. An ENEMY anagram, south of Arabia.
8. A nation which shares Mount Everest with Tibet.
9. An Asian nation that's ALSO an anagram.
10. The nation of Goya, Picasso and Dali.
11. A nation noted for windmills and dykes.
12. A nation that rhymes with the first-ever garden.
13. The nation of kiwis, All Blacks and sheep.
14. A nation whose capital is on an island called Zealand.
15. A nation whose capital is Nairobi.
16. A nation sometimes known as Oz.

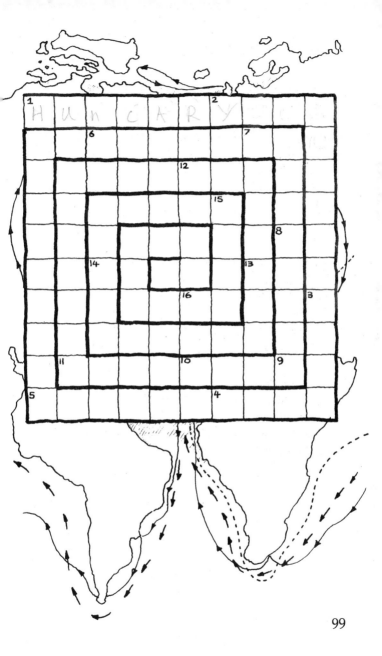

URSINE QUIZ

A quiz for which all you need to know are the bear facts!

1. Which bear lived in a wood under the name of Sanders?

2. What kind of bear, whose Latin name is *Ursus horribilis*, is native to the Rocky Mountains in North America?

3. Was the teddy bear named after (a) Edward Gibbon; (b) Thomas Edison; (c) Theodore Roosevelt; or (d) King Edward VII?

4. Which bear helped to teach Mowgli the law of the jungle?

5. By which two English names is the constellation Ursa Major commonly known?

6. Which bear lives with his parents in Nutwood and has a friend called Algy Pug?

7. Which of Shakespeare's plays includes the stage direction 'Exit, pursued by a bear'? Is it (a) *King Lear*; (b) *The Winter's Tale*; (c) *Romeo and Juliet*; or (d) *The Merchant of Venice*?

8. Which Christian name means, in Latin, 'little she-bear'?

9. In which of C. S. Lewis's Chronicles of Narnia do three Bulgy Bears appear?

10. Which bear lives with the Browns and has a liking for marmalade?

VARIOUS ARTISTS

Can you match all the artists with the works of art which are all their own work?

1.	John Constable	a.	'Charles I on Horseback'
2.	Frans Hals	b.	'The *Fighting Téméraire*'
3.	Sir Edwin Landseer	c.	'Guernica'
4.	Leonardo da Vinci	d.	'The Haywain'
5.	Michelangelo	e.	'The Laughing Cavalier'
6.	Claude Monet	f.	'Mona Lisa'
7.	Pablo Picasso	g.	'The Monarch of the Glen'
8.	J. M. W. Turner	h.	The Sistine Chapel Ceiling
9.	Sir Anthony Van Dyck	i.	'Sunflowers'
10.	Vincent Van Gogh	j.	'Water-lilies'

VESSEL QUEST

This quest conceals thirty-one different vessels –
some ancient, some modern, some large, some
small, but all of them at sea. Can you bring them
shipshape to the surface?

```
E P O O L S C H O O N E R
R E G G U L T R I R E M E
C O R V E T T E U N U S K
L N E S H O Y M A I Q W N
I A T C K G A E D M S H A
P C A N C A W R H S E E T
P Y G G A L L E O N A R R
E R I L M L T U W P L R A
R E R I S E U Q R A B Y W
A J F N A Y G N O C R R L
S U R E T H G I L K I R E
E N I R A M B U S E G E R
A K E T C H A Q S T A F F
```

102

VOWELS ON VACATION

The vowels which ought to be at work in the words below have all, so to speak, g_n_ _n h_l_d_y. Can U (together with A, E, I, and O) bring the vacant spell to an end by putting them back where they belong?

1. _ _RDV_RK
2. _ _R_PL_N_
3. _RCH_ _ _L_G_ST
4. _ _T_M_T_C
5. B_L_ _V_
6. C_R_B_ _
7. D_C_ _V_
8. _ _ST_DDF_D
9. _ _PH_R_ _
10. _ _D_N_

11. K_M_N_
12. K_ _K_B_RR_
13. M_C_R_ _N
14. M_ _ _W
15. _K_P_
16. PH_ _N_X
17. Q_ _ _ _
18. S_P_R_T_
19. S_Q_ _ _ _
20. _N_S_ _L

WHERE IN THE WORLD?

Where in the world would you be if you could see the following ten sights?

1. The Colosseum   _____
2. The Eiffel Tower   _____
3. The Empire State Building _____
4. The Forbidden City   _____
5. The Kremlin   _____

6. The Monument   _____
7. The Parthenon   _____
8. The Sugar Loaf Mountain   _____
9. The Taj Mahal   _____
10. The Wailing Wall   _____

All the answers are to be found among the twenty places named below. When you've chosen the correct ten places, see if you can arrange the initial letters of the other ten to spell something that's everywhere in the world – even though it's nowhere to be seen!

Agra	Honolulu	New York	Rio de Janeiro
Amsterdam	Jerusalem	Oslo	Riyadh
Athens	London	Paris	Rome
Edinburgh	Madrid	Peking	Stockholm
Exeter	Moscow	Prague	Toronto

WHICH DOCTOR?

Across

2. Which lazy-sounding doctor had a parrot called Polynesia?
6. Which doctor lived at 221b Baker Street?
7. Which elegant-sounding doctor was a corpulent cricketer?
8. Which doctor lived in Camberwick Green?

Down

1. Which doctor was no match for James Bond?
3. Which doctor discovered the Victoria Falls?
4. Which doctor had a watery mishap which discouraged him from ever paying a return visit to Gloucester?
5. Which doctor was known to his enterprising friends as Bones?
6. Which doctor was played by William Hartnell originally?

105

WILD ANIMALS AND BIRDS

Can you tame these twenty anagrams?

1. TOGA   GOAT
2. LOVE   _____
3. RENT   _____
4. FOWL   _____
5. TOAST _____
6. GREET _____
7. LATE   _____
8. SHORE _____
9. BRAZE _____
10. CORDON _____

11. LIMNER _____
12. BRAWLER _____
13. PELTER _____
14. SKELTER _____
15. EVICT   _____
16. HIKERS _____
17. OCTAVE _____
18. GARBED _____
19. PAROLED _____
20. CHAINED _____

WORD SQUARES

The answers to the clues can be entered either across or down in these two magic squares. There are no *FOUR BY FOUR* tricks here – but see if you can see why the second square is rather more magical than the first.

1.

1	2	3	4
2			
3			
4			

2.

1	2	3	4
2			
3			
4			

Clues
1. The sun's one
2. Kind
3. Copies
4. What's left

Clues
1. They're used by fryers
2. Region
3. A gaseous element
4. What's found on the beach

XMAS QUIZ

1. Who is known in some parts of the world as Kris Kringle?

2. According to tradition, what were the names of the three wise men who brought gifts of gold, frankincense and myrrh to the infant Jesus?

3. Which word beginning with Y means the season of Christmas?

4. Who thought Christmas was humbug until some spirits changed his mind?

5. 'Good King Wenceslas looked out
   On the feast of Stephen'.
   On which date does the feast of Stephen fall?

6. Under a sprig of which plant is it customary for people to kiss at Christmas?

7. Which King of England was crowned on Christmas Day?

8. What is the title of Clement Clark Moore's poem about strange events on December 24th?

9. How many birds, according to the song, did my true love send to me on the seventh day of Christmas?

10. Can you explain why ABCDEFGHIJK-MNOPQRSTUVWXYZ is another way of writing Christmas?

X-WORD PUZZLE

All the words in the solution have one thing in common – a thing so plain that there's no need to explain any more.

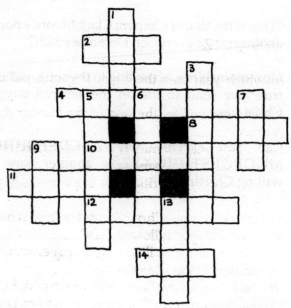

Across

2. A chopper
4. Something that may cause deafness
8. To persuade
10. A female water-spirit
11. Saxon blue
12. In Coleridge's poem, the place where Kubla Khan decreed a stately pleasure-dome
14. To annoy

Down

1. A fence that keeps in cattle

3. To go beyond the limit
5. An extra building
6. Like the people in Madame Tussaud's
7. Slack
9. Truce!
13. The summit

YEARS QUIZ

1. In which year was the Great Fire of London? _____

2. Which year will be the first of the twenty-first century? _____

3. How many years of marriage are celebrated on a ruby wedding anniversary? _____

4. Which year is the title of a book by George Orwell? _____

5. According to the Christian reckoning, which year immediately followed 1 BC? _____

6. In which year did William the Conqueror commission the Domesday Book? _____

7. In which year of the Second World War did the D-Day landings in Normandy take place? _____

8. I was born in the only year of the twentieth century which reads the same even when it's turned upside-down. In which year was I born? _____

9. 'In _____ _____ ___ _____-___,
   Columbus sailed the ocean blue.'
   Can you fill in the missing year?

10. Which letter makes a year long? _____

YOUNGSTERS

Match the youngsters with the adults they'll grow up to be.

1. Calf	a. Salmon
2. Cub	b. Deer
3. Cygnet	c. Hare
4. Duckling	d. Swan
5. Fawn	e. Elephant
6. Joey	f. Fox
7. Kid	g. Rabbit
8. Kitten	h. Kangaroo
9. Leveret	i. Mallard
10. Parr	j. Antelope

YOUR TURN NOW

Turn one word into another by spelling the first word backwards.

Example: Turn the present into what a trophy is.
Answer: NOW, WON.
Now it's your turn.

1. Turn a fool into metal. _____, _____
2. Turn a sailor into one who deserts a sinking ship. _____, _____
3. Turn an implement into money. _____,
_____

4. Turn a Greek god into a canal. _____, _____
5. Turn a thong into pieces. _____, _____
6. Turn a knight of the Round Table into a Tibetan ox. _____, _____
7. Turn a boast into clothing. _____, _____
8. Turn a light beer into what a king is. _____, _____
9. Turn a mosquito into a biting flavour. _____, _____
10. Turn a limb into a jelly-like solution. _____, _____
11. Turn a sea-bird into sea-birds. _____, _____
12. Turn pudding into what hair may be. _____, _____
13. Turn a big bad animal into a stream. _____, _____
14. Turn a heath into space. _____, _____
15. Turn a stopper into a hasty swallow. _____, _____

113

Every answer begins with the letter Z.

1. Crazy: Z_ _ _
2. Nothing: Z_ _ _
3. Member of a South African tribe: Z_ _ _
4. A stringed instrument: Z_ _ _ _ _
5. A gentle breeze: Z_ _ _ _ _
6. Bluish-white metallic element: Z_ _ _
7. The father of the apostles James and John: Z_ _ _ _ _ _
8. The highest point: Z_ _ _ _ _
9. A country formerly called Southern Rhodesia: Z_ _ _ _ _ _ _
10. Like the lines in the letter Z: Z_ _ _ _ _

ZODIAC CROSSWORD

'Heavens above!' I hear you cry – 'not another unclued crossword!' Fear not, however, for the horoscope foretells not too much scope for horror here. All you have to do is enter into the diagram the names of the twelve signs of the zodiac. Take care to avoid any ill-starred conjunctions; only one configuration of the twelve will fit the pattern to perfection. Good luck!

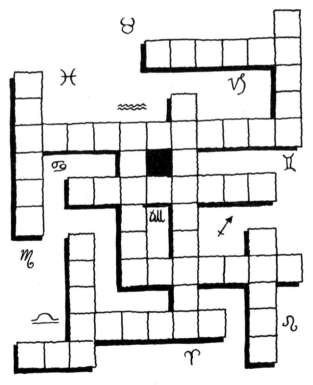

ZOO QUEST

Forty-two animals, most of which might be found in a zoo, are prowling up and down and to and fro inside this cage of letters. Forty-one of them are in contact with at least one of their fellow captives; but the forty-second is untouched by any of the others. Which is the animal that all the rest are avoiding – and why?

```
C A M A L L C N O S I B A
H R T D I P I N O B B I G
Y I A N P O V R R A E B N
E H P A A R E L Y N X A U
N A I P K C T A B M O W N
A T R A O U B U F F A L O
E E Z N A P M I H C R T O
L E I T L I O N U P Y O C
K H M H A N H T O L S L C
R C I E L E P H A N T E A
E A N R U M E L E M A C R
G T K N U M P I H C U O B
I K N U K S I A M O O S E
T H O O R A G N A K A Y Z
```

Answers

ALPHABETICAL WORD-QUEST

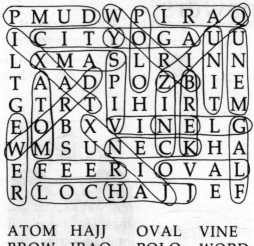

ATOM	HAJJ	OVAL	VINE
BROW	IRAQ	POLO	WORD
CITY	JINX	QUIZ	XMAS
DUMP	KERB	REEF	YOGA
EWER	LOCH	SPIV	ZINC
FLAG	MENU	TAXI	
GLEN	NECK	UNIT	

ANAGRAM ANSWERS

1. NIGHT
2. CONIFER
3. NEVER
4. CANOE
5. RESPECT
6. CREATION
7. MAIDSTONE
8. TREASON
9. RECIPES
10. SCHOOLMASTER

AS I WAS GOING . . .

106.
Although every son had seven sisters, it would be wrong to count seven sisters for every son. This is because each group of seven sons would share the same seven sisters. In other words, each wife had seven sons and seven daughters.

In sum, therefore, I had met:

1	man
7	wives
49	sons and
49	daughters,

making a total of 106 people.

On the other hand, if every son's seven sisters were not full sisters but half-sisters, having the same father but different mothers, then the correct answer might be:

1	man
7	wives
49	sons and
7	daughters,

a mere 64 people.

So now you can see why I'm still so puzzled! If you worked the answer out as 106, take full marks. If you worked it out as 64, take a degree in higher mathematics!

ASTRONOMY QUIZ

1. Jupiter
2. Light
3. Nicolas Copernicus
4. Aurora Borealis
5. When the Moon passes between the Sun and the Earth, blotting out the light of the Sun
6. Orion
7. Halley's Comet
8. The distance travelled by light in a year (nearly six million million miles)
9. A black hole
10. The Sun (The second nearest is Proxima Centauri, more than four light-years away)

BATTLES

1. c
2. g
3. e
4. j
5. a
6. i
7. d
8. f
9. b
10. h

BIRD QUEST

```
Y B B O H G U O H C A L G E
T R E K C E P D O O W L N L
E H L I N N E T T O R U I E
M A G P I E L L C T E G W R
U W B O F R N I U G N E P T
D K S L F O L A R R O R A S
N I T R A M A U L O R U L E
I I J A Y H C R Q E B E T I K
F N R A C S K I W I H L S R
F A L C O N O B T N S U N O
U W I D G E O N I E E V I T
P S N E V A R W O R R A P S
L E G D I R T R A P O D N E T
```

BLACKBIRD	KITE	ROBIN
CHAFFINCH	KIWI	ROOK
CHOUGH	LAPWING	SNIPE
COOT	LARK	SPARROW
CURLEW	LINNET	STARLING
EMU	MAGPIE	STORK
FALCON	MARTIN	SWAN
GULL	OWL	TERN
HAWK	PARTRIDGE	VULTURE
HERON	PENGUIN	WIDGEON
HOBBY	PUFFIN	WOODPECKER
JAY	QUAIL	WREN
KESTREL	RAVEN	

BLACK OR WHITE?

1. White	6. White
2. Black	7. Black
3. Black	8. White
4. White	9. Black
5. Black	10. White

BOOK QUIZ

1. Roald Dahl (the books are *Charlie and the Chocolate Factory* and *Charlie and the Great Glass Elevator*)
2. Professor Branestawm (in stories by Norman Hunter)
3. Eeyore
4. Sherlock Holmes (in *The Hound of the Baskervilles* by Arthur Conan Doyle)
5. *The Hobbit* by J. R. R. Tolkien
6. Toad (in *The Wind in the Willows* by Kenneth Grahame)
7. Manchester
8. Peter Rabbit (in the tale by Beatrix Potter)
9. Peter, Susan, Edmund and Lucy
10. Oliver Twist (in the book of the same name by Charles Dickens)

CAPITAL ANAGRAMS

1. ROME
2. OSLO
3. LAGOS
4. TUNIS
5. PARIS
6. NAIROBI
7. LIMA
8. SEOUL
9. ATHENS
10. MANILA
11. KABUL
12. CARACAS

COL'S COLLECTION

1. COLT
2. COLE
3. COLLIER
4. COLUMBUS
5. COLONIST
6. COLONEL
7. COLOSSUS
8. COLLAPSE
9. COLLEAGUE
10. COLANDER
11. COLLISION
12. COLUMN
13. COLORADO
14. COLOBUS
15. COLLYWOBBLES

COUNTY QUEST

AVON
CHESHIRE
CORNWALL
CUMBRIA
DEVON
DORSET
DURHAM
ESSEX
HAMPSHIRE
KENT

LANCASHIRE
LINCOLNSHIRE
NORFOLK
SALOP
SOMERSET
SUFFOLK
SURREY
SUSSEX
WARWICKSHIRE
YORKSHIRE

CROSS-NUMBER PUZZLE

Across

B.	366	D.	21	F.	1605	H.	49	I.	20000
J.	11	K.	969	M.	007	N.	1910	P.	1918
R.	42	T.	20	V.	1485	W.	186000		

Down

A.	1666	B.	360	C.	64000	E.	101	G.	52
J.	1704	L.	999	N.	180	O.	1588	P.	144
Q.	125	S.	200	U.	10				

DAYS QUIZ

1. 14 February
2. 1440
3. *The Day of the Triffids*
4. Saturday (named after Saturn)
5. Shrove Tuesday
6. It will rain for the next forty days. (St Swithin's Day is 15 July – and the superstition is usually proved wrong!)
7. Thursday
8. Mayday
9. They are the feast days of the four patron saints of the British Isles. 1 March is St David's Day; 17 March is St Patrick's Day; 23 April is St George's Day; and 30 November is St Andrew's Day
10. All of them!

DEFINITION ALPHABET

A.	g	K.	w	U.	s
B.	i	L.	y	V.	e
C.	m	M.	u	W.	b
D.	o	N.	d	X.	f
E.	j	O.	l	Y.	v
F.	h	P.	k	Z.	c
G.	p	Q.	a		
H.	t	R.	x		
I.	z	S.	n		
J.	r	T.	q		

DOUBLETS

Many doublets, like the CAT into DOG example, can be achieved in more than one way. The following solutions, which may differ from yours, are given simply to show that all the changes can be made in the number of steps suggested.

1. BOY into MAN:
     BOY
     1. BAY
     2. MAY
     3. MAN

2. FOUL into FAIR:
     FOUL
     1. FOIL
     2. FAIL
     3. FAIR

3. RISE into FALL:
   RISE
   1. RILE
   2. FILE
   3. FILL
   4. FALL

4. HAIR into BALD:
   HAIR
   1. HAIL
   2. HALL
   3. BALL
   4. BALD

5. DRY into WET:
   DRY
   1. WRY
   2. WAY
   3. WAD
   4. WED
   5. WET

6. LOSS into GAIN:
   LOSS
   1. LASS
   2. LAWS
   3. LAWN
   4. LAIN
   5. GAIN

7. PIGS into PORK:
   PIGS
   1. PINS
   2. PINK
   3. PICK
   4. POCK
   5. PORK

8. HEADS into TAILS:
   HEADS
   1. HEARS
   2. HEIRS
   3. HAIRS
   4. HAILS
   5. TAILS

9. WORK into PLAY:
   WORK
   1. WORD
   2. WOAD
   3. GOAD
   4. GLAD
   5. CLAD
   6. CLAY
   7. PLAY

10. GIRL into LADY:
       GIRL
    1. GILL
    2. GALL
    3. PALL
    4. PALS
    5. PADS
    6. LADS
    7. LADY

EASY CROSSWORD

Across   **Down**
1. Ever   1. Expense
2. Eel
3. Epee

ELIZABETH, EMILY OR ESTHER?

1. Esther   6. Elizabeth
2. Emily   7. Emily
3. Elizabeth   8. Emily
4. Elizabeth   9. Esther
5. Esther   10. Elizabeth

ENGLISH TEST

1. GEL	13. SIN	25. SING
2. GHI	14. GLEN	26. HINGE
3. GIN	15. ISLE	27. INGLE
4. HEN	16. LENS	28. NEIGH
5. HIE	17. LIEN	29. SHINE
6. HIS	18. LINE	30. SINGE
7. LEG	19. LING	31. SLING
8. LEI	20. NIGH	32. SINGLE
9. LIE	21. SHIN	33. SLEIGH
10. NIL	22. SIGH	34. SHINGLE
11. SEG	23. SIGN	
12. SHE	24. SINE	

EXPEDITIONS QUIZ

1. Roald Amundsen
2. Robert Falcon Scott
3. The *Golden Hind*
4. Neil Armstrong, when he became the first man to set foot on the Moon
5. Jason
6. The Jumblies
7. Henry Morton Stanley (The doctor he found, as you may have presumed, was David Livingstone.)
8. Portuguese
9. Because that was the day when they became the first men to reach the summit of the highest mountain in the world, Mount Everest
10. Winnie-the-Pooh

EYE-RHYMES

The real rhymes are:
1. COLLEGE, KNOWLEDGE
2. CONCISE, TWICE
3. DISGRACE, CASE
4. FAHRENHEIT, HEIGHT
5. MALICE, PALACE
6. PEAR, HEIR
7. QUAYS, EXPERTISE
8. REPEAT, DECEIT
9. REPHRASE, WAYS
10. WEDGE, ALLEGE
11. WEIGHT, GREAT
12. WEIR, HEAR

FILM QUIZ

1. *Hans Christian Andersen*
2. The Tin Man
3. Oliver Hardy was always saying it to Stan Laurel
4. *E.T. – The Extra-Terrestrial*
5. *The Great Muppet Caper*
6. Humphrey Bogart
7. Chewbacca
8. *Dumbo*
9. Frankenstein's monster (*not* Frankenstein himself!)
10. Bashful, Doc, Dopey, Grumpy, Happy, Sleepy and Sneezy

FIRST DIVISION

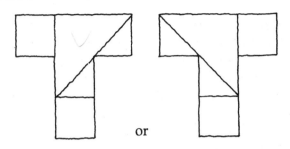

or

FISH QUEST

BARBEL	HADDOCK	RUDD
BASS	HAKE	SALMON
BLENNY	HALIBUT	SCAD
BREAM	HERRING	SHAD
BRILL	LING	SHARK
CARP	MACKEREL	SKATE
CHAR	MULLET	SMELT
CHUB	MUSSEL	SOLE
CLAM	PERCH	SPRAT
COD	PIKE	STURGEON
DAB	PILCHARD	TENCH
DACE	PLAICE	TROUT
EEL	RAY	TUNA
GAR	ROACH	TURBOT

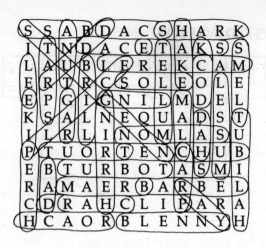

FOUR BY FOUR

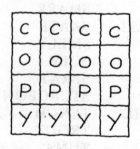

The words represented by the across answers are:
Seas,
Owes,
Peas,
Wise.

GATECRASHERS

1. TOMORROW. The others are all words which begin and end with the same letter.
2. LINKS. The others have none of the five vowels.
3. OUTSIDER. The others have all five of the vowels.
4. BUY. The others all sound like letters of the alphabet.
5. ALLY. The others can all take the suffix SHIP.
6. TROUGH. The others rhyme.
7. HAMMER. The others can all be made into different words by being spelt backwards.
8. RANGE. The others can all take the prefix TELE.

GEOGRAPHY QUIZ

1. Ben Nevis (4,406 feet high)
2. Tasmania
3. Alaska (which is also the furthest north of the States)
4. China (with a population, in 1980, of 964 million)
5. South America
6. The Severn (220 miles long – which makes it ten miles longer than the Thames)

7. Italy
8. The five Great Lakes of North America
9. Wales
10. The Dead Sea

GREAT CROSSWORD

Across	Down
3. Catherine	1. Scott
5. Ape	2. Herod
6. Dane	4. Expectations
8. Bear	7. Eastern
9. Alexander	8. Britain
12. Lakes	10. Sea
13. Tom	11. War
14. Harry	

HIS AND HERS

1. HISTORY
2. HERO
3. THISTLE
4. CHERRY
5. WHIST
6. GRANDMOTHER
7. WHISKERS
8. TEACHER
9. HISPANIOLA
10. CHEROKEE
11. MONARCHIST
12. FEATHERWEIGHT
13. CHISEL
14. SHERLOCK HOLMES
15. APHIS
16. THERMOMETER

HOMONYM HUNT

1. ATE, EIGHT
2. PLACE, PLAICE
3. SHAKE, SHEIKH
4. ALOUD, ALLOWED
5. PEAR, PAIR
6. GNU, KNEW, NEW
7. PRAISE, PRAYS
8. FLEA, FLEE
9. BAY, BAY, BAY, BAY
10. SCENT, SENT, CENT
11. ROAM, ROME
12. CLEAVE, CLEAVE

HOW MANY?

1. One thousand
2. Fifty
3. Five
4. Ten
5. Thirty-two
6. Four thousand
7. Twelve
8. Ten thousand
9. Nine
10. Thirty-nine
11. Six
12. Two

IN OPPOSITION

1. IMPOSSIBLE
2. ILLEGÍBLE
3. IRRESPONSIBLE
4. INVISIBLE
5. IMMEASURABLE

6. NON-FLAMMABLE (not INFLAMMABLE, which actually means the same as FLAM-MABLE!)

I.S.

1. Absent, or absence, without official leave
2. British Broadcasting Corporation
3. Central Intelligence Agency
4. Distinguished Service Order
5. European Economic Community
6. Financial Times
7. Greenwich Mean Time
8. His (or Her) Royal Highness
9. Independent Television News
10. Justice of the Peace
11. Knock out; kick off
12. Luncheon voucher
13. Ministry of Transport
14. National Society for Prevention of Cruelty to Children
15. Oxford English Dictionary
16. Please turn over
17. Queen's Park Rangers
18. Royal National Lifeboat Institution
19. State Registered Nurse
20. Territorial Army
21. Unidentified flying object
22. Video tape recorder
23. Women's Royal Voluntary Service
24. Youth Hostels Association

ISLANDS

1. Anglesey
2. Isle of Man
3. Skye
4. Isle of Wight
5. Cyprus
6. Majorca
7. Corsica
8. Crete

JAMES, JOHN OR JOSEPH?

1. John
2. James
3. John
4. Joseph
5. John
6. Joseph
7. Joseph
8. James
9. James
10. John

JEWEL QUEST

AMETHYST
AQUAMARINE
BERYL
CARBUNCLE
CHALCEDONY
CHRYSOLITE
DIAMOND
EMERALD
GARNET
HYACINTH
JADE
JASPER
ONYX
OPAL
RUBY
SAPPHIRE
TOPAZ
TURQUOISE

JUST JOKING

1. Because Birmingham has only one B
2. Oslo (Czech OSLOvakia)
3. A carpet
4. On the inside
5. 2.30 (tooth 'urty!)
6. Edam
7. A theatre stage
8. Because the other forty are Lent
9. A lemon tree (elementary!)
10. Three – a left ear, a right ear, and a wild front-ear!

KEY WORDS

1. TURKEY
2. HOCKEY
3. DONKEY
4. LACKEY
5. FLUNKEY
6. JOCKEY
7. WHISKEY
8. KEYSTONE
9. MICKEY
10. DISC-JOCKEY
11. MONKEY
12. SOCKEYE
13. WOOKEY
14. HOOKEY
15. MILTON KEYNES

KINGS QUIZ

1. Charles I
2. King David
3. King Canute
4. The King of Diamonds
5. William II
6. Billie-Jean King
7. Louis
8. Henry VIII
9. Richard III
10. King Kong

KNIGHTS OF THE ROUND TABLE

1. BEDIVERE
2. GALAHAD
3. GAWAIN
4. KAY

RELEGATION
LEGUME
ILLEGAL
ELEGANT
LEGERDEMAIN

CESS
CELLENCY
ESITY
YENNE
IGY

LINES

he ceiling.
s he went.
ch worse than his barks.
ry – can it?
arked Lisa, wittily.

LITERATURE TEST

1. AIL	30. TEE	59. TEAT
2. AIR	31. TIE	60. TIER
3. AIT	32. TIT	61. TILE
4. ALE	33. TUT	62. TILT
5. ALT	34. ALIT	63. TIRE
6. ARE	35. EARL	64. TREE
7. ART	36. ETUI	65. TRUE
8. ATE	37. LAIR	66. UREA
9. EAR	38. LATE	67. AERIE
10. EAT	39. LEER	68. AIRER
11. EEL	40. LIAR	69. ALERT
12. ERA	41. LIER	70. ALTER
13. ERE	42. LIRA	71. EATER
14. ERR	43. LIRE	72. ELATE
15. IRE	44. LURE	73. ELITE
16. LEA	45. LUTE	74. IRATE
17. LEE	46. RAIL	75. LATER
18. LEI	47. RATE	76. LITRE
19. LET	48. REAL	77. RATER
20. LIE	49. REEL	78. RELET
21. LIT	50. RITE	79. RELIT
22. RAT	51. RULE	80. RETIE
23. REE	52. TAIL	81. RULER
24. RET	53. TALE	82. TILER
25. RUE	54. TARE	83. TITLE
26. RUT	55. TART	84. TITRE
27. TAR	56. TAUT	85. TRAIL
28. TAT	57. TEAL	86. TRAIT
29. TEA	58. TEAR	87. TREAT

88. TRIAL	110. TITLER
89. TRIER	111. TURRET
90. TRITE	112. TURTLE
91. TRUER	113. ATELIER
92. ULTRA	114. EARLIER
93. UREAL	115. ITERATE
94. UTILE	116. RATTIER
95. UTTER	117. RATTLER
96. ARTIER	118. RELATER
97. ATTIRE	119. RETIRAL
98. ELATER	120. RETREAT
99. LATTER	121. RETRIAL
100. LETTER	122. REUTTER
101. LITTER	123. RUTTIER
102. RATTER	124. TITULAR
103. RATTLE	125. TRAILER
104. RELATE	126. TREATER
105. RETAIL	127. TUTELAR
106. RETIRE	128. UTTERER
107. RITUAL	129. LITERATE
108. TEARER	130. RETAILER
109. TILTER	

LUCKY DIP

1. (d)	6. (c)
2. (c)	7. (d)
3. (b)	8. (b)
4. (b)	9. (a)
5. (a)	10. (c)

MAGIC SQUARES

1.

4	9	2
3	5	7
8	1	6

2.

13	2	3	16
8	11	10	5
12	7	6	9
1	14	15	4

MIXED FRUIT AND VEGETABLES

1. PLUM
2. PARSLEY
3. SWEDE
4. PEACH
5. LEEK
6. LIME
7. DAMSON
8. MANGO
9. HARICOT
10. TANGERINE

MONEY MATTERS

1. h   2. j   3. e   4. a   5. i
6. b   7. d   8. c   9. g   10. f
11. To the right.
12. The suit costs £107.50, and the tie costs £7.50.
13. Five. (One cucumber costs 30p, therefore five can be bought for £1.50.)

5. LEEK

RAMS

URMA
COTLAND
DENMARK
NEPAL
ALGERIA
WITZERLAND
RAN

NATURE TRAIL

April the ninth
It was pretty late, a light breeze blew, and overhead a shimmering haze lay across the sky. Two walking fishermen, Marcel and I, nets in our hands, wandered towards our camp. 'I only caught a blue-bellied pair,' I sighed. 'Not so bad, Gerry,' Marcel muttered. 'I landed a rusty arrow, a feather, one enormous egg, and a beer can too.' The arrow, anyway, is a crisp arrow,' I said. His face darkened. 'I'm allowed to grouch, aren't I?' he growled. 'Ye wouldn't if,' I began – but swallowed my words in horror. For at that moment, in the south, rushing storm-clouds arose and with urgency pressed towards us. 'Marcel, amble not!' I cried. 'I'm not terribly keen on a night in gale-force winds!' As if in chariots of fire, the two of us ran swiftly, he at heroic speed. 'We'll soon be out of this drab, bitter weather!' he yelled. Eerily, snow dropped from the sky; and Marcel, arching his back, got soaked. At last, to be sure, a gleam of light guided us to a tavern. There we sat down, ravenously hungry, to a delicious meal. 'Marcel,' I said jollily, 'that was a wholly memorable day!'

1. Hen
2. Wasp
3. Teal
4. Dove
5. Ash
6. Hazel
7. Kingfisher
8. Celandine
9. Swan
10. Campion
11. Bluebell
12. Iris
13. Badger
14. Elm
15. Yarrow

livided by five thousand)
MIX

n on a calculator, it looks
) like hELLO

18 (Because A = 1, B = 2,

1. Hen   6. Hawk
2. Wasp   7. King
3. Dove
4. Dove
5. Ash   10. Cam

ODD ONE OUT

1. Whale   (the only mammal – all the rest are fish)
2. Stitch   (all the rest are fielding positions in cricket)
3. Puffin   (all the rest are flightless birds)
4. Inspector   (all the rest are names of artists)
5. Tarantella   (the only dance – all the rest are kinds of pasta)
6. Maxim   (all the rest are musical notes)
7. Matthew   (the only New Testament book – all the rest are in the Old Testament)
8. Pennsylvania   (all the rest are surnames of Presidents of the USA)
9. Flintlock   (all the rest are parts of a horse's body)
10. Venus   (the only goddess – all the rest are names of Roman gods)

OF MICE AND MEN

1. GEESE
2. MOOSE
3. MONGOOSES
4. WOODLICE
5. TALISMANS
6. PHENOMENA
7. DEER
8. LENSES
9. SPECIES
10. PLATYPUSES

OFF WITH ITS HEAD!

1. WASP, ASP
2. BEAGLE, EAGLE
3. SEVEN, EVEN
4. FLUTE, LUTE
5. SWINE, WINE
6. GREEK, REEK
7. DEVIL, EVIL
8. NONE, ONE
9. PIRATE, IRATE
10. PRESIDENT, RESIDENT
11. SQUID, QUID
12. MALE, ALE
13. JILL, ILL
14. WELLINGTON, ELLINGTON
15. ODIN, DIN

ORCHESTRAL QUEST

BASSOON
CELLO
CLARINET
CORNET
CYMBAL
DOUBLE-BASS
DRUM
EUPHONIUM
FLUTE
GLOCKENSPIEL
GUITAR
HARP
HARPSICHORD
LUTE
OBOE
PIANO
PICCOLO
PSALTERY
SAXOPHONE
TRIANGLE
TROMBONE
TRUMPET
TUBA
VIOLA
VIOLIN

OUT OF ORDER

1. *TUDOR MONARCHS*
   Henry VII (reigned, 1485–1509)
   Henry VIII (1509–47)
   Edward VI (1547–53)
   Mary I (1553–58)
   Elizabeth I (1558–1603)
2. *ROMAN EMPERORS*
   Augustus (reigned, 27 BC–AD 14)
   Tiberius (AD 14–37)
   Caligula (AD 37–41)
   Claudius (AD 41–54)
   Nero (AD 54–68)
3. *WARS*
   The Hundred Years' War (1338–1453)
   The Wars of the Roses (1455–85)

The English Civil War (1642–51)
The American War of Independence (1775–83)
The Crimean War (1854–56)
The Boer War (1899–1902)
The First World War (1914–18)

4. *ARMY RANKS*
Major-General
Brigadier
Colonel
Lieutenant-Colonel
Major
Captain
Lieutenant

5. *NAVAL RANKS*
Admiral of the Fleet
Admiral
Vice-Admiral
Rear-Admiral
Commodore
Captain
Commander

6. *RAF RANKS*
Air Vice-Marshal
Air Commodore
Group Captain
Wing Commander
Squadron Leader
Flight Lieutenant
Flying Officer

PARTNERS APART

1. ROMEO and JULIET	6. VICTORIA and ALBERT
2. GILBERT and SULLIVAN	7. TOM and JERRY
3. BATMAN and ROBIN	8. TRISTAN and ISOLDE
4. LAUREL and HARDY	9. SIMON and GARFUNKEL
5. PUNCH and JUDY	10. BONNIE and CLYDE

PERPLEXED PEOPLE

1. ALFRED THE GREAT
2. CHARLES DICKENS
3. IAN BOTHAM
4. QUEEN VICTORIA
5. ENID BLYTON
6. WILLIAM SHAKESPEARE
7. NAPOLEON BONAPARTE
8. ARTHUR CONAN DOYLE
9. HANS CHRISTIAN ANDERSEN
10. DANNY KAYE

PLACE NAMES

1. Barking	7. Limerick
2. Cardigan	8. Muck
3. Cork	9. Sandwich
4. Deal	10. Skye
5. Down	11. Wick
6. Lancaster	12. Winchester

And this is how they should be placed:

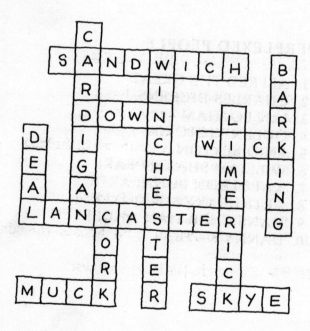

POP GOES THE PALINDROME

1. Bib
2. Civic
3. Deed
4. Deified
5. Ewe
6. Eye
7. Gag
8. Kayak
9. Level
10. Minim
11. Noon
12. Nun
13. Pip
14. Poop
15. Redder
16. Reviver
17. Rotor
18. Sagas
19. Sees
20. Tot

PREPOSTEROUS PROVERBS

1. Too many cooks spoil the broth
2. A rolling stone gathers no moss
3. Birds of a feather flock together
4. A bird in the hand is worth two in the bush
5. Many hands make light work
6. A stitch in time saves nine
7. A friend in need is a friend indeed
8. Every cloud has a silver lining
9. People who live in glass houses shouldn't throw stones
10. He who laughs last laughs longest

QUEENS QUIZ

1. Elizabeth I
2. Boudicca (or, as she is commonly but incorrectly known, Boadicea)
3. Titania
4. Cleopatra
5. The Queen of Hearts, in *Alice's Adventures in Wonderland* by Lewis Carroll
6. Elizabeth II
7. On a chessboard
8. Marie Antoinette
9. Victoria
10. Queen of the South

QUESTIONS OF LOGIC

1. The big Eskimo was the little Eskimo's mother.
2. Five – three ears of corn, and his own two ears!
3. They will both be the same distance from London *when they meet*.
4. Because there were only three of them – grandfather, father and son.
5. Two – the farmer's. All the rest were paws and hooves!
6. A fifty-pence piece and a ten-pence piece. The ten-pence piece is the one that is not a fifty-pence piece!
7. The two men were Siamese twins.
8. It's to be hoped that the *survivors* would not be buried anywhere!

QUOTATION QUOTA

1. The White Rabbit, in *Alice's Adventures in Wonderland* by Lewis Carroll
2. Mowgli, in *The Jungle Book* by Rudyard Kipling
3. Huckleberry Finn, in *The Adventures of Huckleberry Finn* by Mark Twain
4. The Water Rat, in *The Wind in the Willows* by Kenneth Grahame
5. Hamlet, in *Hamlet* by William Shakespeare
6. Peter Pan, in *Peter Pan* by J. M. Barrie
7. Alice, in *Through the Looking Glass* by Lewis Carroll
8. Ben Gunn, in *Treasure Island* by Robert Louis Stevenson
9. Romeo, in *Romeo and Juliet* by William Shakespeare
10. D'Artagnan, Athos, Porthos and Aramis in *The Three Musketeers* by Alexandre Dumas

RATS LIVE ON . . .

1. Rats live on no evil star
2. Don't nod
3. Dennis, I sinned
4. Pupils slip up
5. Name not one man
6. Delia's never even sailed
7. Air an aria
8. Spit slid off a daffodil's tips

NE
NE
E
RN
NNON

RATS LIVE ON ...

MES
R
IS
NT
GA

1. Rats live on no evil st...
2. Dab I nod
3. Dennis sinned
4. Pupils slip up
5. Name not one man
6. Dello saw ...
7. Ar an ...
8. ...

SECOND DIVISION

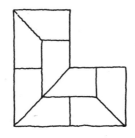

SEMI-SPELLS

1. AMOK
2. BAZAAR
3. DAHLIA
4. ELEPHANT
5. GEYSER
6. GOBBLEDEGOOK
7. IGUANA
8. JODHPURS
9. KERCHIEF
10. LYNX
11. NUTMEG
12. OMELETTE
13. PSALMIST
14. QUAGMIRE
15. RHYTHM
16. SEMOLINA
17. STRENGTH
18. UMBRELLA
19. WIGWAM
20. ZODIAC

SILLY SIMILES

1. As cool as a cucumber
2. As bald as a coot
3. As mad as a hatter
4. As pleased as Punch
5. As old as the hills
6. As happy as a sand-boy
7. As dead as a dodo
8. As good as gold
9. As honest as the day is long
10. As pretty as a picture

SOME SUMS

1. W is 1; E is 5
2. $99 + \%$ (or: $99 + (9 \div 9)$)
3. A, B and C are 1, 2 and 3; D is 6
4. $11 + {}^{11}\!/_{11}$ (or: $11 + (11 \div 11)$)

5. A is 9; B is 1; C is 8
   ```
    999
    111
    888
   ─────
   1998
   ```
6. 888 + 88 + 8 + 8 + 8
7. A is 4; B is 3; C is 7; D is 2; [
   ```
    453
     21
    764
     35
   ─────
   1273
   ```
8. Insert a subtraction sign between the third and fourth number of each set – and the result every time is 333

SPORTS QUIZ

1. Hockey
2. Surrey
3. Golf
4. 27. Yellow = 2, green = 3, brown = 4, blue = 5, pink = 6, black = 7
5. Lawn tennis
6. Aintree
7. Uruguay
8. Croquet
9. The University Boat Race
10. Rugby football (both Union and League)

9. PLANET, PLANE
10. FRANCE, FRANC
11. CODA, COD
12. BADGER, BADGE
13. TEAL, TEA
14. COMET, COME
15. RABBIT, RABBI

6. OSLO
7. LISBON
8. MONTEVIDEO
9. KINSHASA
10. STOCKHOLM

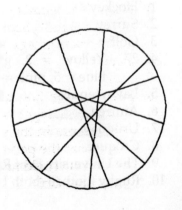

TREE QUIZ

1. The tree of the knowledge of good and evil
2. An oak
3. A deciduous tree sheds its leaves in the autumn, whereas an evergreen is in leaf all the year round
4. Chestnut
5. The hawthorn
6. A cherry tree
7. All four of them
8. Their size – they are dwarf trees
9. The holly
10. Its age. Each ring represents one year's growth

TRUE OR FALSE?

1. True
2. True
3. False   The number varies, depending on the species. Some have as few as fifteen pairs of legs, some as many as 173!
4. True
5. True
6. False   In the first place, George Eliot died in 1880, eight years before T. S. Eliot was born. In the second place, George Eliot was the pen-name of Mary Ann Evans, who could never have been the father of anyone!

7. True
8. False   The Earth is slightly flattened at both North and South Poles.

9. True
10. True
11. False   The most southerly point of Great Britain is Lizard Point.

12. True
13. False   Gustav Holst did compose *The Planets*; but he was English, not Swedish.

14. True
15. False   The line followed by Hadrian's Wall is entirely in England.

UNCLUED CROSSWORD

As you can see, I was thinking along only two lines – one across, and one down!

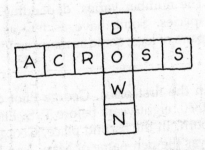

UNITED NATIONS

1. HUNGARY
2. YUGOSLAVIA
3. ALBANIA
4. AUSTRIA
5. AFGHANISTAN
6. NORWAY
7. YEMEN
8. NEPAL
9. LAOS
10. SPAIN
11. NETHERLANDS
12. SWEDEN
13. NEW ZEALAND
14. DENMARK
15. KENYA
16. AUSTRALIA

URSINE QUIZ

1. Winnie-the-Pooh
2. The grizzly bear
3. Theodore Roosevelt
4. Baloo (in *The Jungle Book* by Rudyard Kipling)
5. The Great Bear; the Plough
6. Rupert Bear
7. *The Winter's Tale*
8. Ursula
9. *Prince Caspian*
10. Paddington Bear (in the stories by Michael Bond)

VARIOUS ARTISTS

1. d
2. e
3. g
4. f
5. h
6. j
7. c
8. b
9. a
10. i

VESSEL QUEST

BARQUE
BRIG
CANOE
CLIPPER
LUGGER
PACKET
QUINQUEREME
SCHOONER

CORVETTE	SLOOP
CRUISER	SMACK
DHOW	STEAMER
FERRY	SUBMARINE
FRIGATE	TANKER
GALLEON	TRAWLER
GALLEY	TRIREME
HOY	TUG
JUNK	WHERRY
KETCH	YACHT
LIGHTER	YAWL
LINER	

VOWELS ON VACATION

1. AARDVARK
2. AEROPLANE
3. ARCHAEOLOGIST
4. AUTOMATIC
5. BELIEVE
6. CARIBOU
7. DECEIVE
8. EISTEDDFOD
9. EUPHORIA
10. IODINE
11. KIMONO
12. KOOKABURRA
13. MACAROON
14. MIAOW
15. OKAPI
16. PHOENIX
17. QUEUE
18. SEPARATE
19. SEQUOIA
20. UNUSUAL

WHERE IN THE WORLD?

1. Rome
2. Paris
3. New York
4. Peking
5. Moscow
6. London
7. Athens
8. Rio de Janeiro
9. Agra
10. Jerusalem

You can see what's everywhere, but nowhere to be seen, when the remaining ten places are arranged like this:

Amsterdam
Toronto
Madrid
Oslo
Stockholm
Prague
Honolulu
Edinburgh
Riyadh
Exeter

WHICH DOCTOR?

Across	Down
2. Dolittle	1. No
6. Watson	3. Livingstone
7. Grace	4. Foster
8. Mopp	5. McCoy
	6. Who

WILD ANIMALS AND BIRDS

1. GOAT	6. EGRET
2. VOLE	7. TEAL
3. TERN	8. HORSE
4. WOLF	9. ZEBRA
5. STOAT	10. CONDOR

11. MERLIN	16. SHRIKE
12. WARBLER	17. AVOCET
13. PETREL	18. BADGER
14. KESTREL	19. LEOPARD
15. CIVET	20. ECHIDNA

WORD SQUARES

1.

S	T	A	R
T	Y	P	E
A	P	E	S
R	E	S	T

2.

P	A	N	S
A	R	E	A
N	E	O	N
S	A	N	D

The second square is more magical than the first because it incorporates two unclued words – PROD and SEES – along its diagonals.

XMAS QUIZ

1. Father Christmas
2. Gaspar, Melchior and Balthasar
3. Yule (or Yuletide)
4. Ebenezer Scrooge (in *A Christmas Carol* by Charles Dickens)
5. December 26th
6. Mistletoe
7. William I (the Conqueror)

8. *The Night Before Christmas*
9. 23 (Seven swans, six geese, four calling birds –
   or colly birds – three French hens, two
   turtle-doves, and one partridge)
10. Because the message it expresses is 'Noel' (no L!)

X-WORD PUZZLE

Across	Down
2. Axe	1. Oxer
4. Earwax	3. Exceed
8. Coax	5. Annexe
10. Nixie	6. Waxen
11. Saxe	7. Lax
12. Xanadu	9. Pax
14. Vex	13. Apex

None of the words excludes the letter X.

YEARS QUIZ

1. 1666
2. 2001 (not 2000, which will be the last year of
   the twentieth century)
3. Forty
4. *Nineteen Eighty-four*
5. AD 1 (There was no year nought!)

nd ninety-two
e it turns 'year' into 'yearn'

9. GNAT, TANG
0. LEG, GEL
1. SKUA, AUKS
2. DESSERT, TRESSED
3. WOLF, FLOW
4. MOOR, ROOM
5. PLUG, GULP

ZED AT THE HEAD

1. ZANY	6. ZINC
2. ZERO	7. ZEBEDEE
3. ZULU	8. ZENITH
4. ZITHER	9. ZIMBABWE
5. ZEPHYR	10. ZIGZAG

ZODIAC CROSSWORD

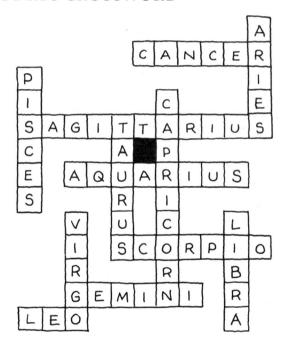

ZOO QUEST

BAT
BEAR
BISON
BUFFALO
CAMEL
CAT
CHEETAH
CHIMPANZEE
CHIPMUNK
CIVET
COYPU
ELEPHANT
ELK
GIBBON
GNU
HIPPOPOTAMUS
HYENA
IBEX
KANGAROO
KOALA
LEMUR
LION
LLAMA
LYNX
MINK
MOOSE
OCELOT
OKAPI
OX
PANDA
PANTHER
PIG
PORCUPINE
RACCOON
RHINOCEROS
SKUNK
SLOTH
TAPIR
TIGER
WOMBAT
YAK
ZEBRA

The animal avoided by all the rest was the skunk –
probably because it stunk!

```
C A M A L L C N O S I B A
H R T D I P I N O B B I G
Y I A N P O V R R A E B N
E H P A A R E L Y N X A U
N A I P K C T A B M O W N
A T R A O U B U F F A L O
E E Z N A P M I H C R T O
L E I T L I O N U P Y O C
K H M H A N H T O L S L C
R C I E L E P H A N T E A
E A N R U M E L E M A C R
G T K N U M P I H C U O B
I K N U K S I A M O O S E
T H O O R A G N A K A Y Z
```

Also in Puffin

WITCHES IN STITCHES
Kaye Umansky

Jokes, interviews, quizzes, health and beauty competitions, songs, poems, lonely hearts, horrorscopes, special offers and much more. Packed with original and totally unexpected fun. If you don't laugh at this you might as well go and do your homework.

ANIMAL MADNESS
Kathryn Lamb

This zoological extravaganza of jokes and cartoons will make you cackle, roar, hoot – even snort with laughter. Prepare to experience the London Lambathon, see the Loch Ness Songster and discover which animal will terrify your aunt.

CREEPY-CRAWLIES
Paul Temple

At last! All you could ever want to know about creepy-crawlies – spiders, worms, caterpillars, centipedes, tadpoles and many more extraordinary creatures. This amusing book is full of amazing facts and fun things to do – build a wormery, create a beehive, spy on pond creeply-crawlies with an underwater scope.

THE PUFFIN BOOK OF BRAINTEASERS
Eric Emmet

Hours of fun await you if you can tackle the problems in this treasure chest of puzzles. Some are simple, some are (almost) impossible, but all are Brainteasers.

CHECK OUT CHESS
Bob Wade and Ted Nottingham

The fun, easy way to learn to play chess. With this book you will easily acquire the sound basic skills necessary for success – many of the exercises have been specially developed by the authors and all tried and tested with beginners.

THE PUFFIN BOOK OF AMERICAN FOOTBALL
Simon Kilner

From tactics to the razzmatazz of the Super Bowl, from the origins of the sport to profiles of the NFL clubs, from college football to the game in Britain, this acclaimed introduction to one of television's most spectacular sports tells you almost everything you could wish to know about American football.

HOW TO SURVIVE
Brian Hildreth

If you ever go hiking, camping, climbing or canoeing – or even if you're just taking a plane or boat trip – this book should be part of your essential equipment. Written by the author of an air force survival handbook, it's an indispensable manual for anyone lost – or risking getting lost – in the great outdoors.